Steven Pressman

Liz Perle, who worked in book publishing as an editor and publisher for more than twenty years, recently joined the nonprofit world, where she is editor in chief of *Common Sense Media,* the nation's leading nonpartisan organization designed to help families make the best media choices for their children. She is also the author of *When Work Doesn't Work Anymore.* Perle lives in San Francisco with her husband and two children.

ALSO BY LIZ PERLE

When Work Doesn't Work Anymore

Additional Praise for *Money, A Memoir*

"Liz Perle is not a traditional financial writer in the school of Suze Orman but rather a keen psychological observer of her own guilt, magical thinking, and emotional dodges when it comes to money."

—*Time*

"Her thought-provoking tract, bolstered by extensive interviews and research, urges women to forget Prince Charming, stop fantasizing about that six-burner Viking stove, and start funding their IRAs."

—*Entertainment Weekly*

"Liz Perle confessess to erratic fiscal behavior in *Money, A Memoir,* bravely exposing her financial foibles and hang-ups. . . . Kudos to her for having the courage to air her dirty financial laundry so other women can benefit."

—*USA Today*

"At once more contentious and more ambitious than the cynical view would have it . . . Perle has good cause to press on, and good instincts about where to press. . . . She backs herself up with psychiatrists and sociologists . . . but she also does the uneasy work, however anecdotally, of unpacking identity and security as functions of dependence and extrapolating the money-influenced issues of power and trust and respect that hang many women, and many men, up. Perle's best material is the really personal, presumably unspeakable stuff. . . . Driven to expose the most shameful, presumably unmentionable aspects of our financial disappointments, with the . . . conviction that frank discussion is essential for progressing beyond them."

—*San Franciso Chronicle*

"Thought-provoking."

—*Chicago Sun-Times*

"Illuminating . . . With candor and self-deprecating humor, she offers herself as Exhibit A. . . . The book contains a message that needs to be heard and heeded, not only to benefit women but also to give their offspring a better financial example."

—*The Christian Science Monitor*

"Intriguing . . . Compelling."

—*The Washington Post Book World*

"A wake-up call for the retail-inclined."

—*Forth Worth Star-Telegram*

"*Money, A Memoir* is a page-turner."

—*Bloomberg News*

"*Money, A Memoir* is written very much on the model of Naomi Wolf or Peggy Orenstein. . . . Perle is so friendly sounding and full of examples that it's hard not to start thinking about your own financial situation as you read. More personal than a self-help book, more utilitarian than a memoir, Perle's book might instead be thought of as a call to arms. Time to get our financial houses in order."

—*The News & Observer* (Raleigh)

"The strength of the book lies in Perle's willingness to 'be the first fool,' to lay out her own insecurities and missteps with total candor."

—*Los Angeles Times*

"[A] remarkable sociological study-cum-memoir . . . Perle's book raises more questions than it answers, which is part of its allure—it'll surely have readers thinking twice before they log on to Bloomingdales.com after a bad day at work."

—*Publishers Weekly* (starred review)

"Eye-opening . . . Perle's interviews with psychologists and financial experts are compelling. Her phrase 'emotional middle class'—to describe what she considers the country's now-mythic middle class—may enter the lexicon."

—*The Buffalo News*

"This wonderful book shines a spotlight on the ambivalence women have about all things financial—we love nice things but feel guilty if we have them and resentful if we don't. I'm making it required reading for all my clients—men and women!"

—Chellie Campbell, author of
The Wealthy Spirit and *Zero to Zillionare*

"Fascinating."

—*San Francisco* magazine

"How did Liz Perle get so far inside women's heads? This is much more than a memoir. It's one of the most insightful and important books about women's behavior I've ever read."

—Hope Edelman, author of *Motherless Daughters*

"If you want to understand many women's complex and contradictory attitudes about money, take out your wallet and buy Liz Perle's very personal and very honest look at the subject in *Money, A Memoir*."

—Myrna Blyth, former editor in chief of *Ladies' Home Journal* and author of *Spin Sisters*

"A smart, funny, insightful book on women and money. Liz Perle writes with love and enthusiasm about this essential topic."

—Judith Orloff, M.D., author of *Postive Energy*

"Change is in the air. Someone finally has the courage to be straight about women's emotional struggles with money. Every woman who reads this touching, smart, and true book will come away with more insight into one of the most important relationships in her life—the one between her and her pocketbook."

—Debbie Ford, author of *The Dark Side of the Light Chasers* and *The Best Year of Your Life*

MONEY, A MEMOIR

WOMEN, EMOTIONS,
AND CASH

LIZ PERLE

PICADOR

HENRY HOLT AND COMPANY
NEW YORK

www.picadorusa.com

Picador® is a U.S. registered trademark and is used by
Henry Holt and Company under license from Pan Books Limited.

For information on Picador Reading Group Guides,
as well as ordering, please contact Picador.
Phone: 646-307-5629
Fax: 212-253-9627
E-mail: readinggroupguides@picadorusa.com

Designed by Victoria Hartman

Library of Congress Cataloging-in-Publication Data
Perle, Liz.
Money, a memoir : women, emotions, and cash / Liz Perle.
    p. cm.
Includes bibliographical references.
ISBN-13: 978-0-312-42627-9
ISBN-10: 0-312-42627-5
    1. Women—Finance, Personal—Psychological aspects—Case
studies. 2. Finance, Personal—Psychological aspects—Case studies.
3. Money—Psychological aspects—Case studies.   I. Title.
HG179.P3664 2006
332.0244'0082—dc22

                                        2005050317

First published in the United States by Henry Holt and Company

First Picador Edition: January 2007

10 9 8 7 6 5 4 3 2 1

FOR STEVE,
DAVID,
AND ROSHANN

From birth to eighteen, a girl needs good parents.

From eighteen to thirty-five, she needs good looks.

From thirty-five to fifty-five, a good personality.

From fifty-five on, she needs good cash.

I'm saving my money.

—Sophie Tucker

CONTENTS

PROLOGUE: MONEY, A MEMOIR

SOMEWHERE OVER THE PACIFIC OCEAN, I REALIZED I'D better count my money. There'd been no time in the airport. I'd been too busy wrangling a four-year-old and wrestling with my own mix of numbness, efficiency, and sorrow. I'd checked my luggage—a box of toys, a suitcase filled with tropical clothes—and turned to see my husband kneeling by his boy, both of them in tears. My son and I were leaving Singapore, where we'd moved five weeks earlier from New York City to join my husband. He'd been working there for six months. But by the time we'd arrived, he'd changed his mind about wanting to be married.

"Please go home," he said, concluding a tearful discussion we'd had during my first week.

I pointed out that this would be tough since we'd sold our apartment, expecting we'd be in Asia for three years.

"Go. Please," he repeated.

Four weeks later, having exhausted any hope of salvaging our marriage, I stood listing against the Singapore Airlines counter as everyone around me scurried purposefully to somewhere or away from someone. I was having trouble focusing on what was happening. In one hand, I clutched two passports, and in the other, a fistful of bills that had been peeled from a thick wad. Snapping to, I stuffed them in my pocket and took my son in hand, pausing before my husband. Do we hug? Kiss? There was no way for our bodies to say goodbye. I mumbled that I'd call from San Francisco when I got to my friend Sue's house, and headed down the gangway to the waiting plane, tugging my bewildered child.

There were fifteen $100 bills.

I had just lost my marriage and my home, and I had fifteen hundred bucks.

SINCE THIS IS a book about money, I won't go too deeply into the losing-the-marriage part. Suffice it to say that the first thing on my mind as I flew thirty-five thousand feet over Guam while headed back to the States was not cash. But putting the heartbreak aside, I did have a few concerns: My companion was a four-year-old, I was unemployed, there was no place called home, and every single household possession I owned was in a sealed container on a huge cargo ship steaming its way toward Asia through the Suez Canal.

For as long as I could remember, I'd lived with a kind of chronic anxiety that something like this would happen. That I'd lose my financial footing and end up shuffling around in bedroom slippers pushing a shopping cart down an alley. On the surface of it, this was not a rational fear. Since I was born a relatively middle-to-upper-middle-class girl with all the privileges, experiences, and options that come with membership in the Club of Disposable Income, the chances of my remaining in one end or another of that income bracket were probably going to be pretty good. (That and the fact that, in my saner moments, I did know that my husband was an unhappily married—not bad—man and that he would not leave me and his son high and dry.) But that hadn't stopped me from worrying that one day, without warning, I could plunge from the safety of my nice life into—if not poverty—a quality of life so diminished that I wouldn't be able to bear it. These stubborn fears had persisted through years of economic independence, and they regularly woke me up at 4:00 A.M. disguised as regret over an unnecessary impulse purchase, sure that it represented the first step on the steep path to sheer ruin.

Then, one day, quite suddenly, my worst fears were realized. Without warning, my marriage collapsed, taking with it my financial security. After all, I had (quite willingly) handed over my economic life to my husband. Now he and all our assets were retreating at five hundred miles an hour.

Here's what was clear: that I wasn't getting my marriage back.

Here's what was not so clear: how I was going to afford my life.

There's nothing like losing just about everything to lay bare what's important.

LONG AGO, AND not entirely consciously, I made a quiet contract with cash. I would do what it took to get it—work hard, marry right—but I didn't want to have to think about it. I simply wanted to know I would be financially secure. This intentional avoidance eventually exacted its price. In the service of sidestepping, whenever possible, my anxious feelings (if not my facts) about money, I've signed over a lot of power to anyone or anything that promised to make me feel financially safe—no matter what the consequences. I've left my emotions about money—the fears and ambivalences—largely unexamined. I've avoided facing my contradictory feelings about the whole subject, such as the fact that I want to have my own money with the independence it gives, while simultaneously hoping someone or something will step up to the plate and take care of me. I've invited these highly emotional and unstable sets of feelings into every relationship I've had, and they have silently accompanied and influenced each one—with my father, my work, my friends, my bosses, and my husbands. (There have been two—oddly, both named Steve.)

My nonspecific fears of financial ruin have led to some good things, too, though. They've pushed me to work hard, which propelled me into some good jobs, which, in addition to nice salaries, gave me a sense of identity, some freedom, and extended periods when I felt pretty good about myself. Anxiety about my future has put money in my IRA, has helped me save enough for a down payment on a house, and, in the hopes that the sins of the parents aren't visited on the kids, has prodded me to impart to my children a respect for cash and a sense of its importance. In fact, I've always paid my way, not just out of financial need but because emotionally I've needed the freedom that a decent income ensured me.

None of these facts, however, made a dent in my anxieties.

My financial solvency—like most things in life—has come with a few strings attached. In order to keep the real and imaginary wolves from my door, I've occasionally acted in ways that haven't made me feel too swell about myself. I've been silent when I should have spoken up. Stayed ignorant when I should have paid attention. I've remained tethered to unhappy and unhealthy work and personal relationships. I've been complicit in bad business practices and poor management.

My agreement to trade bits of myself for security has had personal side effects—eruptions of rebellious immaturity where I haven't paid my bills or lived within my means in spite of very real consequences. I didn't change my IRA portfolio from all those tech stocks I'd invested in hoping to get rich quick (whoops). I didn't balance my checkbook and ended up paying 18 percent interest on the overdraft that bounced over to my Visa card. I've left jobs purely because I've hated them, even though they paid me well. Each of these incidents resulted in big reversals in my financial fortunes, and if you graphed my net worth over the course of my life, it would look like the mark of Zorro. Embarrassed and occasionally unnerved by my own tendency toward erratic fiscal behavior, I've stubbornly refused to examine it, instead choosing to pin my hopes on that white knight, dream job, unknown dead rich uncle, or winning lottery number that would rescue me.

This kind of magical thinking—if not downright denial—has allowed me to maintain a remarkably constant approach/avoidance relationship with this most fundamental part of my life—with the emphasis on avoidance. I'm no stranger to the financial fantasy realm. My daydreaming drew heavily and rather unimaginatively on the run-of-the-mill Disney model. It involved the acquisition of a husband who would present me with a "happily-ever-after" life by taking away my money fears. Yet despite my most strenuous efforts, I didn't manage to find one until my midthirties. Buried inside my increasingly frantic search for he-who-would-be-solvent was the fantasy that once married, I would have the security I craved. Insistent feminist that I was (and remain), I still wanted the option of knowing that I, alone, would not have to be the steward of my financial destiny.

I married the first guy I dated who owned a really good suit. (Okay, to be honest, I also married the first guy who asked.) He was handsome and powerful and had an impressive job. He also made more money than I did, which I admit was a total turn-on. (Well, he had some debts and some overvalued real estate. But I overlooked these departures from the script.) On our first date, he told me to get out of the street and go stand on the curb, that he could hail us a cab. He was an alpha male, a self-made man, and clearly comfortable with finance and investment. I exhaled.

In spite of years of paying my own way, I couldn't hand over the checkbook fast enough. He liked to control the cash, pay the bills, invest the money, and govern the expenses. That was more than fine with me. I had a little money in my IRA, a bit more in a 401(k), and some profits from selling a home I'd bought with a small inheritance from my grandmother. We both had good jobs; we both made good money. He managed it. I spent it. That worked for me. I settled into domestic life all too happy to place my financial future in the hands of someone who would show his love for me by paying for everything.

The dream took some unexpected turns—the first being a period when I was out of work. The balance of power shifted quickly, almost toppling our marriage then and there. But when I found a new job with an even better salary than before, things seemed to even out. But then my husband's company reorganized dramatically as it prepared to go public. He'd worked for this firm for twenty-plus years and had many stock options that would be worth a substantial payout if he stayed on. The only hitch was that continued employment meant we'd have to move to Singapore for three years. Since I now had what I craved—a child and financial security—it only seemed fair to support my husband's part of the dream, which involved early retirement, golf, and general relaxation.

I swallowed hard and painted a pretty picture for myself of a life of adventure. I couldn't hold a traditional job in Singapore (there was no way I would get a work permit), so instead I looked forward to reading the classics, settling into a routine as a full-time mom, traveling, and writing. Except for that earlier three-month period of unemployment, I had never depended on someone else for money, so a part of me wasn't keen on a repeat performance. But there weren't a lot of options, and I figured the dependency wasn't for too long. I trusted that at the end of the trip, we'd have enough money for my husband to do what he wanted, and for me to feel secure. I was more than willing to trade three years of ungovernably frizzy hair on the humid equator for a lifetime of financial ease. My husband transferred our finances, we sold our home, and after a six-month separation—he'd had to move earlier than I could—my son and I packed that box of toys and suitcase full of shorts and T-shirts, and we moved to Singapore.

We already know how that turned out.

So it was that five weeks later, at the age of forty-two, I bumped down on the stormy tarmac of San Francisco International Airport with no job, no home, and no clue what was going to happen. I had those hundred-dollar bills and, as it turned out, a small savings account, but almost everything else—even the joint credit card I carried—was in my husband's name and under his control half a world away.

This could have been my Scarlett O'Hara moment when I turned draperies into finery and pulled my metaphoric carrots from the earth, proclaiming, "I'll never be hungry again!" But that's not what happened. Instead, I collapsed on my friend Sue's sofa with a box of tissues and didn't move much for quite a while. As I lay there, my predicament slowly came into focus. I—who had devoted much of my life to making sure I would be financially safe and secure both through work and marriage—had handed my husband that power and now found my economic stability vanished within a matter of weeks. Just like that, I'd fallen through my carefully crafted safety net.

In my stunned and prone state, something became very clear: I could no longer afford the murky and oblique relationship to money I had maintained for most of my adult life. I had to admit that I held a good deal of responsibility for my situation. It was the price I paid for not wanting to think about my financial state, and it explained how I, an independent woman with twenty-plus years of career behind her, had come to be splayed on a couch in San Francisco, watching as El Niño dumped buckets of water down the steep hills and the gray streets.

MY RELUCTANT EXAMINATION of my convoluted relationship with money began in earnest that day. It ultimately led to conversations with hundreds of other women—Americans, Brits, Australians, Europeans, Chinese, Japanese, Central and South Americans. I talked to women from twenty years old to eighty. I met women online, through financial self-help groups, and through friends of friends of friends. It didn't take much prodding to get them talking. It turns out that when it comes to money, women everywhere have so many fears and fantasies in common. Some differences in behaviors existed due to both generational and cultural differences, but studies backed up my impression that basic similarities existed under these disparities. One 2004 study commissioned by a Japanese investment bank showed that a forty-nine-year-old Japanese woman had the same priority as her forty-nine-year-old American counterpart—saving for retirement because she feared the man in her life took too many risks with money and was putting her old age in jeopardy.[1]

When I would begin an interview, the woman would inevitably start out by sighing really deeply. "Money," she would say, pausing. Then she would tell me that while she didn't care about money for its own sake, she did care about what it could purchase: freedom, peace of mind, identity, social position, a nice life for herself and her family, some good things, and real independence. Not to mention really nice shoes. "How much do you need in order feel secure about those things?" I would ask. The answer rarely wavered; it was some version of "I don't know. All I know is I don't have enough."

It didn't matter what a woman's age was or whether she

lived in a trailer or gated community; when it came to "enough," no two dollars were created equal. Some women believed that $100,000 would solve all their problems, and others were convinced that if they had $1 million, they would experience the same fears, only bigger. "Enough?" one woman echoed when I asked her what number represented that concept. "There's no such thing as 'enough.'"

No matter what a woman's net worth, she was exquisitely aware that her bank balance powerfully affected her sense of well-being. Regardless of their actual assets, women felt plagued by rapidly changing feelings of surfeit and scarcity. Some of the women I talked to were really rich. Others were hovering at the bottom of the middle-class tax bracket. Yet they all admitted that money was the great unexplored territory in their emotional terrain. And in no case did ignorance turn out to equal bliss.

This became particularly evident in a conversation with my friend Alison, a lovely ex-chef in her midthirties who was in the middle of negotiating her financial settlement in her divorce. Her husband had been having an affair. For two years. A fact she discovered when she went to return a really ugly scarf he'd given her and found out he'd bought not one but two of the hideous accessories. Indeed, as she dug through old Visa bills—the ones she had never so much as opened—she realized that this Noah's Ark approach to gift giving had been going on for years. That's how she figured out her husband had a lover. Now she was as hurt and angry as she'd ever been, and she alternated between wanting to rake her husband and his income over hot coals and a more guilt-laden approach—one that centered on blaming herself for having been "such a bitch" (her words) and feeling she shouldn't leave him impoverished because of her character flaws and shortcomings.

Alison asked my advice on structuring child support, division of property, and who should pay for college. She wanted me to help her put a price on mothering and figure out what compensation would be fair for having given up her restaurant career. I'd have been glad to offer help, but I couldn't get her to tell me how much money she thought she needed to live on every month.

"Do you not know? Or do you not want to tell me?" I asked her.

"I do know, and I'm too embarrassed to tell you," she admitted. "What I need and what I spend are two different things."

As I hung up the phone, it struck me that I know more about my friends' sexual assets than their financial ones. They've never hesitated to tell me all about love affairs, dreams, disappointments—even their husbands' most minute physical, moral, mental, and sexual failings—but I have no idea what any of them earn or spend each month.

WHAT IS SO troublesome about our relationship with money that we're so elusive or dishonest about it—to ourselves, to others? When it comes to money, many of us are completely contradictory, often evasive, and irritatingly indirect. We won't ask people about their incomes, yet we peg our social positions by where we *think* we stand comparatively. We disguise our appetites by manufacturing "needs." We never reveal how much money we make, or what we have in the bank. We defiantly spend when we know we shouldn't. We're reluctant (sometimes afraid) to negotiate for better salaries and find it humiliating to haggle over prices. We amaze our husbands, lovers, and friends with reports of the things we bought on sale that never ever were, and we routinely shave a few bucks off the cost of something as minor as a lipstick so we won't appear irresponsible.

Not only that; we've developed a whole moral vocabulary to describe our supposed disdain for money: greedy, miserly, moneygrubbing, gold-digging, dirt-poor, nouveau riche, stinking rich, well-off, well-to-do—the list goes on and on. But we can come up with only a few sympathetic descriptors: self-supporting, independent, generous . . . self-made and enterprising can cut both ways. These adjectives reflect our emotions about money: greed, envy, guilt, even shame. It turns out we feel that liking money is somewhat immoral.

We need money and resent the fact that we do. We want it, we like to spend it, and we know that just admitting that qualifies us as potentially superficial and materialistic people. We may condemn our wants as crass consumerism, yet we can be stopped dead in our tracks at the thought of losing our lifestyles. We regularly want more than we can afford, which leaves us in a semipermanent state of deprivation.

Buffeted by alternating currents, we either engage in debt-defying impulse spending or plunge our heads in the sand in an effort to drown out our financial anxieties.

We can deny that money matters to us as much as we want, but then how do we explain the degree to which we've endowed it with all sorts of superpowers that can transform our emotional states? We've granted it the authority to single-handedly make us feel safe and cared for. We twist ourselves into impossible shapes to please and stay attached to the people and institutions that dole it out. Put it this way: If we behaved at work, with our friends, or with our husbands as indirectly, ambivalently, dishonestly, dependently as we do with money—we would immediately go into psychotherapy.

When it comes to our concerns about cash, we live in a land caught between our fears and our appetites. What do we do with this money anxiety? For many of us, our response has been a kind of voluntary blindness. We don't mind making money. We don't mind being in charge of our financial destinies. We just don't want to have to *think* about it too much.

This twisted relationship—and the guilt, embarrassment, reluctance, and avoidance that are involved—can have some serious consequences. In the course of my research, I heard stories from women like Amanda, a nurse who felt so badly about leaving her ten-year marriage to her first husband (who would routinely loan her car, her clothes, her books, and her jewelry to others because, after all, he said, he paid for them, and so they were his to give) that she didn't ask for a dime. She had so much baggage around money, she said, that she didn't want to face the fight and put a price on her life with him. Rather than ask for alimony, she enlisted in the army to pay for her college education. Now, as a single mom with a set of young twins, she can be called into conflict at any minute. Or women like Nancy, a stay-at-home mom who entertained lavishly in a beautiful home that she renovated or redecorated every five years but who hadn't had sex with her husband in ten.

Although I met some women who were truly direct about and in control of their finances, most of the rest of us clearly aren't. More women will file for bankruptcy this year than will graduate from college,[2] suffer a heart attack, or be diagnosed with cancer. More than half of all retired women live in poverty. A family with children is 75 percent more likely to be late paying its credit card bills, and according to the work done by Harvard's Elizabeth Warren and Amelia Warren Tyagi, the single biggest predictor that a woman will end up in financial collapse is the birth of a child.[3]

So with all this at stake, why is it that so many of us don't just "get over it"—as my friend Carole suggested to me one morning over coffee—and deal with our money issues? Why do perfectly brilliant and sensible women admit that their eyes glaze over when individual household budgets and broader financial matters are discussed? Why the drive to spend beyond our means, why the willed insecurity about investing? Why the inability to ask to be paid what a job is worth? Why do we want to earn money and still be "taken care of" by someone else?

I did meet women who, usually because of big reversals due to big debts, divorce, death, or illnesses, had come to grips with their financial demons. Some attended seminars; others bought books by the pound that told them more or less the same things: make a budget, learn about investments, be proactive. These books promise to catapult us from our present paycheck-to-paycheck life into the stratosphere of the most wealthy and privileged. Who wouldn't want to be a millionaire?

But for many of us, these self-help tools backfire. There's no surer way to feel woeful about our financial situations and our financial prowess than to compare our bank accounts and fiscal habits with those of the most disciplined, wealthy people in the world. These personal finance books often seem like an extension of the ads and magazine articles boosting cellulite-reducing creams and ab machines. They all imply we're inadequate on some level. (Otherwise, why would we need their products?) Just below the surface they send the subtle message that whatever we have, whatever we've saved, it's not enough. Almost all the women I spoke to seemed pretty susceptible to these messages of insufficiency and their subtext of peril.

OF COURSE, THERE are women who are very comfortable with money, who happily and intelligently handle not only their own finances but also those of their families and their corporations. They either had never experienced or had moved beyond an emotional relationship with money. When I began my inquiries, I had assumed these would be the younger women, those who had grown up in an age of post-feminist fiscal equality. And there were some who fell into that group. But for the most part, it was maturity and experience that created harmony and acceptance, not time and place of birth. The women I found who had the healthiest relationships possessed an honesty and a clarity about what money could and couldn't do for their lives. They'd managed to unpack their emotions from their finances, and they took care of themselves with confidence. They were able to bring the same understanding to money that they had brought to issues with their families, their weight, their work, and even their love lives. Their stories inspired me, but, I admit that at first I felt a little out of my league. Yet by the end of my investigation, I began to grasp a little bit of their peace of mind.

I guess that's why this book started out as a memoir—one of money as much as my mercurial relationship with it. Because for me, there's no better way to examine life's troublesome questions than through the show-and-tell of others' experiences. Because all the theory and how-to books either scared me, or shamed me, or, to be honest, put me to sleep. Because I'm not the kind of person who has ever had a lasting transformation from a self-help book. Yet. Because I pay very close attention when other women talk honestly about sex, relationships, alcohol, spending, eating, or anything else that falls into the marginally compulsive category. Because I found that when I confessed my fears and idiosyncrasies to other women, theirs came tumbling out as well. It turns out that when money is the topic, most of us need permission to talk about it because we've been taught that it's not a suitable topic of conversation. And because, finally, I feel a hint of hopefulness when I listen to someone who has made all the mistakes I have, along with a few more that I have yet to sample.

This is not a book of financial advice. Just like the women in this book, I worry about money and wrestle with it daily. I experience these concerns from ground level, eyeball-to-eyeball with the rising and sinking cash levels in the checkbook. I'm writing this book precisely because I'm *not* a financial expert or a psychologist, but because I have covered a lot of financial ground.

I've been rich, and I've also been poor (and as Sophie Tucker famously quipped, "Rich is better"), and I've inhabited most points along the middle-class spectrum. I've married a wealthy man and one a bit more "fiscally challenged." I've enjoyed years of financial stability, a few of downright largesse, and some that were a little too much on the rocky side for my taste. Now, as I approach my middle-aged years, just when I thought I'd have a modicum of security, I still live paycheck to paycheck, wondering if I've saved enough to support myself in my old age. I'm a woman, like the women in this book, who has spent a lot of time thinking about what makes us truly independent emotionally, spiritually, physically, and yes, fiscally.

So I'm putting my experiences down on paper with the

full knowledge that I'm one of the most fortunate women in the world. I've enjoyed the benefits of a great education, supportive family, and excellent career opportunities. Make no mistake; I consider my financial fears a privilege. I am acutely aware that the tyranny of choice is not even a pale shadow in the face of the tyranny of need. And I feel guilty, like so many women I have spoken with, that I have so much and still feel so anxious.

My hope is that this book will encourage women to take a look at their own complicated feelings about money and what money means to them. Perhaps that way we can move closer to liberating ourselves from the fears and fantasies that keep us from asking to be paid what a job is worth, or from saving for our retirement, or that leave us mired in intractable debt. As long as we let emotions influence—even dictate—our financial lives, we remain prey to unhealthy, at times destructive relationships. Until we honestly dig into some contradictory and even unattractive feelings and behaviors, we will continue to live with this equation of *ambivalence + avoidance = anxiety.* We will continue to enter into relationships that we dress up as love or need and that are, fundamentally, economic contracts. Without consciousness and understanding, we will continue to trade away parts of ourselves in our quest for an elusive feeling of security, locking us into what one woman called "the never-ending path to *more.*"

I often tell my kids that the secret to happiness is wanting what you have, not having what you want. But first we need to know what it is we really want "more" of. So much of what we desire involves money and what it can buy. And so much doesn't. Without understanding which is which, we will find ourselves looking to money to give us something that it cannot possibly purchase.

· 1 ·

SECRETS AND LIES

THE ONLY TIME I EVER HEARD MY ELEGANT GRANDMOTHER use a Yiddish word, I was nine years old. Sitting on one of the twin beds in her bedroom (it had been years since she'd slept anywhere near my grandfather), I watched her search through one of her bureau drawers as she kept up an uninterrupted monologue detailing her version of the facts of life. These had nothing to do with biology, but with an unwritten but inexorable code of behavior to which all young women must militantly adhere. My mother had died a year earlier, and ever since that bewildering August day, I had been the regular recipient of tokens of my grandmother's philosophy: white gloves, random costume jewelry, a sanitary napkin belt that looked like a medieval torture device, embroidery lessons, and other flotsam that reflected her sense of what a girl needed in order to survive and triumph. Mostly this involved serious training in the art of becoming a marriageable young woman (that being the end goal of everything).

This day, she was on a tear. Drawers opened, stockings shoved aside, scarves pushed into corners, each new thrust released the scent of Chanel No. 5. Her search took on a kind of urgency I hadn't seen before. Finally, she pulled out a strange and tiny woven metal sack from the bottom of a drawer of underwear. The object fit in her hand and seemed to be made of spun gold. It had some kind of cap on the top and a pin so a woman could securely attach it to her clothing.

"It's a reticule," she said, opening the mouth of this misshapen and minute bag. Seeing my completely blank expression, she continued. "It's something a woman wears to keep her valuables hidden."

This I had never seen.

My grandmother went over to her pocketbook, a black patent leather rectangle with a silver clasp that I liked to snap open and shut. She removed a $20 bill, folded it twice, and stuck it into the bizarre purse, which she then handed to me.

"This is the beginning of your *knipple*," she said, pronouncing this alien word "kah-nipple." "It's a woman's private stash. Every woman needs one. A just-in-case account. Every woman needs money of her own that her husband never knows about. So she can do what she wants. What she needs. Remember that."

Long after my grandmother died, I recalled this

conversation and its promise of secrecy and peril. It would be thirty years, though, before I would really understand what she meant.

SO IT WAS that before I learned the facts of life, I was instructed in the facts of money. Money would take care of me. I should do whatever it took to get some and squirrel it away. Money would come from my husband and possibly protect me from him at the same time. With it, I would be safe. But this path to security was indirect, extremely secret, and very, very important.

I received one other explicit money instruction from my grandmother. It had to do with not talking about it. On one of my frequent afternoon visits spent playing with the earrings and necklaces in her white leather jewelry box, I asked her if she and my grandfather were rich or poor. "You never talk about money," she pronounced. "It's private."

End of story.

In my grandmother's hierarchy of what mattered in life, money silently reigned. She believed that at the end of the day, a woman's safety and security (not to mention social position) depended on it. It clearly didn't matter by what desperate or devious means a woman acquired this money—just so long as she had it. But God forbid anyone should talk about it. This big important thing that would be so critical to my safety and freedom.

Until a few years ago, my grandmother's message sat

pristinely in my gray matter, intact and unexamined, largely because I wasn't even aware of its presence. But that didn't stop her perspective from informing my thinking. Sure, my understanding of money and income had been updated. On the surface, I behaved like a financially responsible and frequently rational fiscal creature. I worked, saved, and paid my bills (well, most of them). Experience had taught me that my grandmother was right—that with my own income, I was sovereign over my life. But emotionally, my feelings about money's importance hadn't advanced much. Unfortunately, my stubborn refusal to look at these feelings led to occasional outbreaks of indirect, often manipulative behavior around people who could supply cash, erratic episodes of compulsive spending followed by anxious hoarding, and a general and omnipresent lack of trust about who could best provide for me.

WHETHER WE WANT to admit it or not, each of us has a relationship to money that goes beyond the getting and spending. Money is never just money; it's our proxy for identity and love and hope and promises made and perhaps never fulfilled. It's our social sorter. It's the ticket to our dreams. Yet there's a conversational force field around the topic that repels discussion. "Don't count your money in front of the poor," a friend once snapped at me after I'd mentioned how much I'd paid for a leather skirt. For the life of me, as I looked around, I couldn't see the poor person to whom she was referring. But all these many years later I can still feel the sting of humiliation at being exposed as insensitive, selfish, and greedy. Few topics are as guilt inducing and taboo as this one.

Our silence doesn't serve, however. It seals in dubious advice (like my grandmother's), allows outdated moral prejudices to persist (money is filthy lucre)—not to mention gender roles (it isn't ladylike to be materialistic)—and protects serious social inequalities like the fact that men and women remain unequally compensated for the same jobs. The need to be secretive robs us of a way to examine our ambivalent feelings about our materialistic and emotionally dependent attitudes and impulses. Silence shields us from seeing how, unconsciously, we broker invisible deals to make sure we get what we want and stay safe and secure. And it keeps us from examining the toll those agreements exact. Finally, our silence means women can't be released from the low-level and often undetected feelings of anxiety, guilt, envy, anger, hunger, and fear that money inspires.

There's nothing I want as badly that I'm more ashamed of wanting than money. No wonder I don't like to talk about it. Yet how will I ever address my relationship with this forbidden subject if I don't?

WOMEN RELATE TO money much differently than men do. There are many reasons large and small why this is true. When I ask Stephen Goldbart, a prominent psychotherapist and codirector of the Money, Meaning, and Choices Institute, about these differences, he tells me that they are ancient and deeply embedded psychologically and biologically in both sexes. These differences are so old, so deep, and such a part of our basic wiring that they cannot be ignored. "There are strong gender differences when it comes to money—differences of identity and of historical roles. For men, the interplay of money and love and power has not really changed in thousands of years; they have always been the providers, and their identities and power come from this old survival-based role."

Goldbart has spent years observing how both men and women commingle money and power, which, he says, they need to do in order to survive. While men directly equate money and power, women, who have traditionally had no access to money, combine the two in a very particular way that has a lot to do with romantic love.

"Historically, money was melded with being provided for and taken care of. Thus it's a challenge for women to separate out love and money," Goldbart points out. "The degree to which a man provided for a woman has been her sustenance and her life. Therefore, for a woman, a man's success and his sharing of that success financially is more than just what we see in her lifestyle. On an unconscious level, it has to do with knowing that she and her children will survive. When we talk about money, we're talking about providing for basic human needs; this is basic human wiring. And while these providing and dependent roles have changed in the last seventy-five years, to brain stem psychology, that is no time at all."

The way we're raised also has much to do with the different approaches men and women have to money. Somehow I sincerely doubt my grandmother pulled either of my male cousins into her boudoir and handed them a secret sack with a $20 bill in it. They weren't told that their social and financial security would be determined by their marriages or that talking about money was "not done," immoral, selfish, tacky, or just plain bad manners—quite the contrary. Joline Godfrey, the CEO of Independent Means and author of *Raising Financially Fit Kids,* reassures me that my family experience is far from unusual. Godfrey, a financial educator, feels that our culture remains stuck in the belief that we must take care of girls. She observes that we still expect too much from boys financially and too little from girls, and explains that for boys, the issue around money is shame because money is more directly tied to their manhood, whereas womanhood is still very much connected to a girl's beauty and to her ability to connect to others in relationships. Godfrey believes it is easier for women to disconnect from financial responsibilities because our identities aren't at stake if we do. But for boys and men? Money and providing determine their feelings of self-worth.

My male cousins understood quite clearly that they'd be judged by their abilities to go out, club the money dragon over its head, and haul home that cash. Holiday dinner conversations centered on what happened in the stock market, other people's (lousy or lucrative) investments, football, and "Did-you-see-the-Shermans'-new-Vista-Cruiser?-Someone-must-be-doing-well" observations of others' good or ill fortunes. We all absorbed the import of these conversations, but as in most families, the emotional impact of these messages differed depending on whether you were the girl cousin or the boy cousin. All of us learned that money would determine our social standing and whether or not we were perceived to be "successful." Indeed, we all went on to have good jobs and good careers. But looking around the table, it was clear for the girl cousins that we had two paths to this achievement: We could get there by work or by marriage.

For the most part, men know that society sizes them up rather two-dimensionally by how much they do or don't make. Most (if not all) men grow up with the lurking suspicion that the job description of "manly man" still includes the task of being the classic "provider." "How do men rank their self-esteem?" Goldbart asks. "By their productivity in the world and whether or not they are successful. Most men would still define success in terms of their work and their finances first and their families second." Goldbart feels that the way men view their purpose and judge their value remains unchanged by the fact that women now contribute to family income. "There was a women's—not a men's—revolution," he concludes.

Although this bottom-line assessment of a desirably successful man is broadening in tiny increments to include the unquantifiable (and uncompensated) nurturing skills of fatherhood, men still understand that their very worth is measured by their financial prowess. They think—and not unjustly—that women evaluate them by how much wealth they can create and how much money they can provide. This is something women don't like to admit they do, but Pamela York Klainer, a financial consultant and the author of *How Much Is Enough?* has seen it for years in her clients. "Many men tend to want to exaggerate their differences through money. Someone has to be 'top dog,' 'alpha man.' It's clear that men use money as a differentiator. They will show their power by buying expensive gifts for those around them to show that they have 'made it.' It's a form of power. Whereas women will use money to form bonds and friendships."

But it's different with women. We may keep a beady eye trained on the wardrobes and kitchen appliances of those around us, but part of keeping pace with our friends lies in the fact that we don't want money to separate us. Put six women together in a room with a range of incomes, and all will find a safe middle ground in order to minimize our differences. We intuitively know that nothing divides us faster than money.

Where men use money as shorthand to determine who has the power in a relationship, women will let it be a surrogate for love and attention. This frequently shows up in divorce settlements, where, as Stephen Goldbart has seen, a woman will want a certain amount of money because, psychologically, that money represents all the love the husband didn't give her. In this way money compensates for emotional disappointments.

Obviously, a continuum of these money behaviors exists on which women and men inhabit both ends of the spectrum and all points in between. But the gist of their comments is clear: With money, men do more than provide; they create social and political hierarchies. They draw their power and position from these fiscal disparities. (It doesn't even have to be their own money. All they need is access to it and the power to dispense it.) But women will downplay their financial differences for the sake of harmony and connection out of the basic female biological and psychological drive to be connected to other women in order to feel safe and to survive. We do this even if it means denying or minimizing our fears and desires.

I have one friend I'll call Magda, whom I admire deeply. She's one of the smartest women I've ever met. She's nononsense, and she tells it like it is. We enjoyed (and still do) one of those friendships where we could and did tell each other everything, knowing we would call each other on anything where we were kidding ourselves.

Then she inherited $60 million.

I would be lying if I said her windfall had no effect on me. I started walking on eggshells around her for fear she might think I was her friend only because she was so damn rich. At the time, I was mid-divorce, still homeless, sleeping on the lower half of my best friend's youngest daughter's leftover bunk bed. Magda's sudden abundance short-circuited me for a while. My first thought on hearing of these astronomical millions was "Gee, can't she spare one of them? She'd never miss it, and I could really use it." The truth is, all I could see was her wealth and my neediness. Her money mirrored back my own emotional feeling of scarcity. I was ashamed of these feelings, and our friendship became, for a time, stained by the secret I now kept from her—that of my envy and my fear of how she'd suddenly see me.

As Cyndi Lauper sang, "Money changes everything."

THE THERAPISTS OLIVIA Millan and Karina Piskaldo take these observations one step further. "Men are raised to see the world as hierarchical and competitive," they say. "There's always a one-up and one-down position, a winner and a loser. Women see the world as cooperative and democratic; they share. In addition, they are allowed—even encouraged—to be needy and vulnerable, while men are discouraged from such display." [1]

These may be gross generalizations, but that doesn't make them any less true.

Needy and vulnerable. Two red flags that create a state of alert in me. I don't want to be either one of those things. I don't know a single one of my girlfriends who wants to be one of those things either. But as I push aside my irritation at the adjectives, underneath I feel a bit caught out. Needy and vulnerable apply to me more than I would ever like to admit. In fact, it's precisely my fear of being either one that has done the most to spur my economic autonomy. Yet it's exactly these two qualities that are my inheritance, because I learned how to be a woman from someone who, like all her ancestors, had to depend on men to survive.

It's as simple as this: On the one hand, as a creature of the postwar, baby-boom, women's-movement times of the latter half of the twentieth century, I grew up defining myself as an independent, self-supporting woman. I don't even question it. It's my identity, it's my economic reality, and it's my right. I depend on my independence.

And yet there's still that other part of me—the one that wants to reserve the option of depending on someone else. That ancient desire may have primitive roots in survival, but it also feels familiar. Growing up in my mother's and grandmother's worlds, I learned that part of being a woman meant taking care of the children and home while husbands took care of the financial security. In that world, it feels normal to maintain the illusion of financial dependency. It's a place where I can step away from my worries about whether I am smart enough or interested enough to properly invest my IRA or whether I have enough rainy-day money set aside for when I'm laid off or fired. Because I have often confused care with cash, there have been times when, sitting in the middle of a semicircle of income tax forms, I want nothing more than to pack it all in and let someone else show me how much they love me by taking away all my financial burdens.

Besides, women worry about money more than men do. A survey conducted by *Redbook* magazine in conjunction with *Smart Money* magazine found that fully one out of every three women classified themselves as worriers, versus less than one in five men.[2] Much of this has to do with our legacy as women and the fact that, for most of recorded history, we weren't allowed to have money of our own. (In many cases, we *were* the money.) Instead, our currency involved beauty, strength, health, and the ability to reproduce like bunnies. Because we were forbidden to own or inherit property, our path to financial security lay through men. The better we were at the womanly arts of nurturance and care, the more attractive we were. The larger our fathers' fortunes and thus our dowries, the better our chances were of survival and safety. Law and custom ensured that we had to depend on men, institutions, or families to provide for us. We did whatever we could to be safe and guarantee our children's safety. We learned to trade ourselves for cash in the most direct of ways.

But in the last fifty years, all that changed. Sofia, a nurse in her midforties, remembers growing up in the 1970s in New York. "My mother was a part-time switchboard operator; my father was a bartender. I watched my mother beg my father for money as he lied about where his paycheck went. He drank and gambled, so sometimes nothing was left even the day he got paid. But as I was growing up with all this, the women's movement was going on in the background, and it informed my feelings about how I was going to be as an adult. I swore I would never be a victim like my mother. All of a sudden, there were alternatives."

Any woman born after the end of World War II experienced an explosion of role models, whether or not she or her mother actively participated in the women's movement. The simple fact that women began to gain economic independence and equal status was enough to thoroughly upend the economic model that had been the norm for the middle class. Suddenly, women's lives and financial realities changed radically—but much of the rest of how we defined and valued ourselves as women did not. No revolution erased my grandmother's admonitions or my mother's stay-at-home-wife life or those brain cells of mine that at age six recorded Cinderella singing, "One day my prince will come."

Reconciling roles and expectations hasn't been so easy for Claire, a tall, stunning brunette in her early thirties. She's on her third "career" (speech pathologist) and digging out from credit card debt from "career" number two (Internet writer). "I was raised not to think about money, and then there was this vicious backlash where I was supposed to generate it," Claire says with an edge in her voice. "We weren't rich or anything. I went to public schools and had to babysit and all that. But we weren't poor either. My mother stayed home and raised us. Until I was in my teens, I never saw her earn a cent. Instead, it seemed that money flowed in and out and wasn't a big issue," she remembers. "Then one day it became clear that to be a success in my parents' eyes, since I hadn't gotten married to a handsome, rich man, I had to earn a certain income. I've never felt I've measured up to their expectations, even though I kind of blame them for not clueing me in earlier."

Claire felt a sense of betrayal when she realized she was completely unschooled in how to take care of herself financially. As a girl, she watched as her father drilled her older brother on the need to make money. "Your sisters will get married, so they will be okay," he would say to Claire's only brother. "But you're going to have to make it on your own." Claire shakes her head as she remembers this. "My sisters and I never got that message. It was assumed that someone would take care of us."

When Claire was in high school, her mother started teaching. "She wasn't terribly interested in business, but she liked to shop, and she liked not having to ask my father for money," she recalls. "But really, I saw two very different approaches to money growing up." Now Claire is trying to navigate between the two roles. "It's left me with a real love/hate thing when it comes to money. I need to make a living, but part of me resents the fact that it isn't ever going to be for me like it was for my mother."

"We are still at the very beginning of a huge transition in sex roles, and the result is confusion," Stephen Goldbart observes when I tell him about the women I'd talked to who, like Claire, felt both unprepared and torn between historical gender roles. "The outcome of this confusion is anxiety, identity confusion, and depression. Obsession with money can also be a symptom of the difficulty of feeling solid in one's identity. All this," he concludes, "makes it all the more urgent for women to come to terms with their money issues."

ALL I HAVE to do is take a look at my own family tree to see how rapidly financial roles have changed. Two generations back, my maternal grandmother catapulted out of poverty by marrying my grandfather. When we were little, she would tell the story of her marriage as though it were a fairy tale. "I was a great beauty," she would tell her granddaughters (the rest of the sentence went, "too bad none of you inherited anything from me"). "Your grandfather fell in love with me at first sight." From there, the story went downhill rapidly since it turned out that, while they lived a materially comfortable life, they never really liked each other very much. But never mind, the lesson went, make yourself as beautiful and as marriageable as possible so that you have financial means.

One generation ago, my mother went to college (something my grandmother never would have dreamed of for herself), married my father, found a job, but stopped working when I was born in the mid-1950s. She, like most middle-class women, expected that she'd depend on my father for money. When my grandmother took over for my mother, she taught my cousin, Ginger, and me how to cross-stitch so we could embroider our eventual husbands' pillows and hand towels. According to her script, this dubious (actually ludicrous) talent would ultimately convert into marriage and, thus, financial security. But within fifteen years of my first sampler, I assumed something she'd never dreamed of: that I would be my husband's full and equal financial partner.

That's a lot of territory to traverse in a few short decades—from financial dependency to self-sufficiency, indirection to direction. In the 1950s, the number of women who outearned their husbands was so small that the information wasn't even systematically gathered. But fifty years later, almost one in three women do and our numbers rise every year.[3] We control $4 trillion in yearly consumer spending. We make 62 percent of all car purchases. We take 50 percent of all business trips. We control more than 50 percent of all personal wealth in this country.[4] And we do this while shouldering the majority of family responsibilities. We've gotten caught in a time warp where our economic realities have changed faster than our expectations and identities.

We may be the first generation to experience widescale economic independence, even as old behaviors die hard. We keep quiet about any pride we take in the money we earn for fear of losing not only our feminine appeal but also the relative high moral ground on which we base our sense of un-materialistic identity. It's no longer our parents who silence us. We've taken over the job ourselves. We give ourselves the mixed message that money is simultaneously vitally important and something we shouldn't show we care about. Or if we must, it should be in the service of caring for our families.

The fact is that we are caught between two different identities and value systems when it comes to money. As Lois Frankel states in her book *Nice Girls Don't Get Rich,* "On the one hand, we're taught about the value of money and the need to spend and save it wisely. On the other, we're implicitly or explicitly taught that it's equally important to be kind, nurturing, and collaborative; that our real roles revolve less around money and more around relationships."[5] This double set of money instructions follows us into every situation—work, love, family—and, because of the mutually exclusive nature of these two paths, ensures that no matter what, we feel we've done something wrong with every money decision we make.

Most of us go to work every day in rigid environments that were designed for and by men—ones that our presence hasn't changed all that much. It's not surprising that the making of wealth is prized in that environment since that's how men have historically judged their success. But this definition causes a real conundrum for women. In a landmark study on women's quality of life conducted by the Whirlpool Foundation, women overwhelmingly concurred that money and materialism were too important in people's lives. They felt that "materialism, greed, and selfishness increasingly dominate American life, crowding out a more meaningful set of values centered on family, responsibility and balance in their lives." While women weren't "anti" money, those studied felt it should be brought into proportion with "the nonmaterial rewards of life."[6]

The disconnection between a material measurement of our success and a more relational, spiritual one creates a painful emotional conflict for women, one that shadows everything we do. Ask a woman about what truly defines her, and money rarely enters into the equation. But ask her about the center of her worries, and money is always present. A 1995 study by the Merck Family Fund that examined women's work/life balance issues succinctly summed up the problem: "Women are deeply ambivalent about wealth and material gain. While we decry the crass materialism of our society and its consequences, we also want 'success' for our children and ourselves. Most people express strong ambivalence . . . they want to have financial security and live in material comfort, but their deepest aspirations are non-material."[7]

Ten years later, the impact of materialism shows up on our emotions. Too much focus on the material can lead to depression, which makes sense if a good deal of our time is spent worrying about what we can and can't afford. When we think about everything we want or what we could have if we only had the money, it necessarily leaves us in a hungry state of mental deprivation. Yet we also must devote time and energy to making money and caring for ourselves financially, or dire consequences result. As we try to balance these material needs and material desires, we must constantly negotiate between these competing urges, even if we don't realize it. "Any conflict can create tension and anxiety," says Louann Brizendine, a psychiatrist and the director of

the University of California's Women's Mood and Hor-
mone Control Clinic. "And we all naturally want to avoid
those feelings. It's no wonder we don't like to focus on something that leaves us feeling so unsettled." And, according to
Brizendine, women experience depression more than twice
as much as men do.

THERE'S ANOTHER ANXIETY that often stops our investigation of our relationship with money: Nothing worries us
more than the fear of going broke. Anne Richards, the former governor of Texas, once said that her number one
worry was ending up living in a trailer in her daughter's
driveway. When I asked women about their top five night-
mares, winding up a bag lady featured in almost all their
scenarios, right along with not having enough money to
retire safely. Yet when I asked those same women how
much time they spent focused on investing for their retire-
ments, almost all of them said either that they didn't have
any money to invest or that they left the management of
what they had to husbands or professionals.

Here's something that keeps us up at night, that we
spend most of our days trying to procure, that we don't care
about for its own sake, and about which we either lie with
regularity or are completely silent. And too often our
response to the conflicted feelings we have is to avoid taking
care of ourselves. We bury our feelings at quite a price, however. The fact is that we spend more on face cream and shoes

than we do on our retirement funds. Women routinely don't save enough to survive on when we become widows—which 50 percent of us will be by the age of sixty.[8] Women still earn only 78 percent of what men earn for the same jobs,[9] and only a third of us have positions that even offer retirement plans.[10] And because about half of all working women take time off at some point in our work lives to care for our families, the value of what retirement funds we do have is lowered even further by these interruptions.[11] Sometimes the only way to do everything on our plates is to cut back to part-time work. So it doesn't come as a great surprise that 61 percent of all part-time workers are women with little or no access to 401(k) plans.[12] More than 58 percent of female baby boomers have saved less than $10,000 in a pension or 401(k) plan.[13] Between one-third and two-thirds of women now thirty-five to fifty-five years old will be impoverished by age seventy.[14] The average female born between 1946 and 1964 will likely be in the workforce until she is seventy-four years old due to inadequate financial savings and pension coverage and will not have the resources to maintain the same standard of living she had prior to age sixty-five.[15]

No wonder we get anxious about the whole subject.

LIKE THESE WOMEN, I want to know the money is there. I want to know I won't be on the street at seventy. But I have no desire to read *Barron's* or follow the stock market. To say

I'm contradictory or irrational on this topic severely skirts the issue. I'm in plain old denial.

These fears were my real inheritance from my grandmother. According to her, I wasn't supposed to have to worry about all this. According to her, it was my right as a woman to be cared for, or, if I wasn't, to have secretly cared for myself. But when I had to re-create my life from scratch, it became clear that I literally couldn't afford those ideas anymore. I realized that all that time, I'd been toting around more than a $20 bill in that little sack she gave me. Her very value system was pinned to my metaphoric undergarments. But I no longer had a choice about opening up that magic bag and examining the silent instructions, prejudices, and values it held.

· 2 ·

THE EMOTIONAL MIDDLE CLASS

THE FIRST TIME I CONSCIOUSLY ACKNOWLEDGED THAT my relationship with money had more than a few emotional kinks in it was on a September morning in 1994. I was loitering in bed enjoying one of the few side benefits of having been laid off from my job. I could hear the water running in the next room; my then husband was shaving. As soon as I figured the coast was clear, I slipped out of bed and tiptoed over to the bureau, where his wallet was sitting on top. I stealthily slid a $20 bill out of his billfold and walked to my closet, where I quickly stuffed it into the toe of my sneaker. Instantly horrified, I recognized the cringing, shameful feeling as the same one I used to get in junior high when I would pinch a few bucks from my dad. But that didn't stop me from repeating my petty theft—until I amassed close to $400. My money fears were so powerful that they plowed right past all my moral stop signs.

I had been out of work for long enough that I'd begun to panic about what the future held. My marriage wasn't in the greatest shape, and with each swipe of the credit card, I felt more deeply dug into emotional debt to my husband, who had complex feelings of his own about suddenly being cast in the role of sole provider. The week before, he'd made a crack about the size and scope of the Visa bill, causing me to go on an immediate and determined money-starvation diet.

It lasted four days.

Up to that point, I had always prided myself on the fact that I was a woman who didn't care about money or material possessions. I had congratulated myself on my superior resistance to the call of the designer bag and the shoe-of-the-moment club. The only problem was, that superiority turned out to be a total fiction. I did care about money. Very deeply, I discovered. But I'd disguised that truth by spending in ways that looked selfless: making a beautiful home, buying presents for family and friends, and entertaining. I had passed many hours discussing with my friends the problem of balancing work and family, where I usually staked out the high moral ground of advocating for having fewer possessions, working fewer hours, and spending more time with family.

That philosophy was fine except that it quickly went out the window the moment I lacked the cash to do what I wanted. In this case, it was to buy my husband a fancy birthday present, a painting of my husband, my son, and me happily picking apples in an orchard on a fall day. I wanted to give him the image of the marriage I wanted to have—make it concrete, put it on the wall for everyone—well, mostly him—to see.

For this, I stole his twenties.

AS SOON AS I went back to work and had an income again, I pushed the specifics of this humiliating episode into the shady corner of my mind I reserve for the memories that make me really uncomfortable. I happily focused on the demands of my new job, serene in the knowledge that I could go to the cash machine and withdraw money for groceries and expenses and not feel guilty about freeloading off my husband.

I don't know what happened to the painting. When my husband and I separated, it got crated up and sent away with half our possessions. But I do know that I ultimately held on to something of tremendous value, even if it took a few years for the importance of it to sink in. That incident showed me that when it came to money, I'd been kidding myself. It mattered much more to me than I was willing to admit. As long as I earned a decent salary, I hadn't needed to look at what it meant to me. I hadn't had to stop and think deeply about it. Either there was enough, or there wasn't.

But the real nature of my relationship with money had—if only momentarily—become unpleasantly clear. Sure, I needed it, but this larcenous episode wasn't caused by a budget deficit. My hungry theft came from a much deeper and more conflicted place—a tangled dependency of safety and love and cash—that I wasn't remotely interested in facing. I had become accustomed to and defined by a lifestyle that I was clearly willing to do just about anything to maintain—even at the expense of my principles.

When had this happened? When had I come to depend on *things* to define and support me? Growing up, as I did, in a small town at the outer edges of commuter land, I didn't think that money or things were all that important. In fact, I didn't really focus on money at all. It was simply there. We weren't rich. We weren't poor. In this 1950s neighborhood, we were all the "Joneses," and everyone more or less kept pace with one another. The Bates kids, the Reynolds, Nobles, and Calendars—we rode sherbet-colored bikes with tassels trailing from the handgrips. We begged for Barbie dream houses for our birthdays and sang in the Christmas pageant with the real, live sheep every year whether or not we were Christian. We progressed in lockstep; when the Campbells got a color TV, others soon started popping up in adjacent houses, spreading like some strain of consumer goods virus. But I never dreamed of having a pony or something so big that no one else in my town had one. Instead, I looked to my left and my right, gauging my expectations to what I saw others had determined as reasonable and possible.

Like my friends, I went to a decent public school, where I was encouraged to do well, attend college, and go as far as my talents and brains and hard work could take me. In this,

I was no different from many Americans. Didn't the American dream make us affluent with expectations, opportunities, and promises, if not always with cash? We felt we were given a cultural promise: that if we worked hard, we could have the lives of our dreams. With this expectation came a strange sense of entitlement: It was our right to pursue life, liberty, and happiness and—while we were at it—a promised land of comfort and surety. And what better way to purchase those things than with money?

"We have definitely monetized the American dream," says Juliet Schor. "Certainly, you have an equation in society that money equals happiness, that it equals security, that it equals success—and that's connected to happiness. Freedom. Independence. Pretty much all of the key positive values of American culture. All of them have a very strong link to money. Money is seen by many people as the mechanism for getting those things."

The American dream found its muse in the latter half of the twentieth century's economic middle class. In the 1960s and 1970s, we elevated it—with the help of a voracious mass media—to an almost iconic level. In the flush of the postwar economy, suddenly more people could afford more things than ever before. Our fantasies, our possibilities (and our measure of outward success) were displayed in front of us in glossy ads and on television. We made 2.7 children, a car in the garage, and a mortgage more than a goal; we uplifted it to a moral ideal. We exported the middle-class poster children, the *Leave It to Beaver* Cleaver family and Mary Tyler

Moore's Laura Petrie, to countries around the world as the calling card of the land of opportunity. We wanted everyone to see the picture of stability and material comfort that represented the achievements of a generation who fought a world war and had given their children something to show for it.

But by the time their children, the much ballyhooed baby boomers, arrived to claim their piece of this paradise as adults, the middle class had changed. Not the dream but the reality. Working with that same drive that provided our parents their passports to stability and comfort, we pushed for more. In the revolution of rising expectations, what our parents provided no longer seemed like "enough." Middle class stopped being a synonym for security. Instead it signified a perilous portal, on one side of which lurked financial difficulty and on the other an Oz of glimmering wealth. Being middle class now meant living simultaneously with the fear of falling out of it and the dissatisfaction of not being wealthier.

"There is no middle class in this country anymore," Barbara, a trim woman in her early sixties, tells me as we walk through New York's Central Park on a sunny spring day. "Not the one I grew up with anyway. My father was a teacher and my mother worked for the government in personnel, and she never made more than $175 a week for twenty-five years. Yet they were able to take good care of us. We had a car, we took vacations, we had a good education in a good public school, and we had a decent apartment, all on a salary that couldn't keep an immigrant family afloat today.

"This safety has just gone. It's just disappeared. On every block in my neighborhood, you can buy $300 or $400 'dry-clean-only' handmade baby snowsuits. This is the way people live. My son and his wife were looking for baby strollers last weekend, and there's an $800 stroller out there." Barbara shakes her head. She knows they can afford these things since they both work and are making good salaries, but this no longer sounds like middle class to her. It's something else. It's almost the opposite of safety since it's mostly about consuming. We spend to feel safe, but in the spending, we chip away at the ground beneath our feet. We want to make "enough" to live the life we want, but each time we approach "enough," it moves a few acquisitions farther out.

IT'S IRONIC THAT the generation that grew up in this mythic middle class basically killed it in trying to re-create it for themselves. Those of us who are postwar baby boomers may have been aiming for the spiritual values that were the hallmarks of the Age of Aquarius, but we shot right past the principles of love and equality and instead created one of the great materialist orgies in recorded history. You could say that we lost our peripheral vision and stopped looking sideways at our neighbors, who more or less earned what our parents earned, and lived as our families had lived.

Instead, we began looking up, reaching for pieces of luxuries previously reserved for the most wealthy. Their lives entered our living rooms through an omnipresent media and an endless parade of fashion and home-decorating magazines whose job it is to manufacture appetites and sell us more and more things to satisfy them. Luxury teasingly reached down toward us, coming tantalizingly close, and we responded by upscaling our material aspirations and expectations. We turned our kitchens into design centers, our bathrooms into spas. We doubled the average size of our homes.

How could we afford all this? Two reasons: First, women went to work in record numbers, and second, so did the credit card companies. In the last thirty-five years, the number of two-income families has risen to 62 percent of all married couples—up from 39 percent in 1970.[1] In a median-income ($71,000-per-year), two-worker household, the "second" salary provided by the woman (a little more than $20,000 per year) has fueled a consumer boom like no other in history.[2]

Almost all of the growth in household income between 1970 and 2003 came from women. These additional resources were not lost on the marketers and manufacturers. The sudden by-product of this income was what the author Michael Silverstein calls a "mass luxury movement." Nor did this extra income escape the notice of all those banks and lending companies that were so eager to extend us credit. In September 1958, credit cards arrived uninvited in the mailboxes of some sixty thousand residents of Fresno, California. By the end of 1959, there were two million credit cards circulating in California alone.[3] Today, the average monthly U.S. credit card debt is $8,000.[4]

But what about the guilt and discomfort women claim they feel about being so materialistic? "People have come to experience their purchases as 'necessities,'" Juliet Schor explains. "When you buy something that you absolutely need, you are not being materialistic. Materialism is still seen as excessive, but most people don't experience their own consumer behavior as such. Most people don't intend to get into debt, and most people no longer have this idea that debt is somehow a sin or a bad thing. They are willing to take the increased uncertainty to have what they have come to 'need.'"

Endless mail drops of catalogs helped us develop "needs" for coffeemakers that grind the beans fresh every morning or for sheets with thread counts previously reserved for royalty. We marched past the simple desire for comfort to a need for luxury. Each purchase represents a highly textured transaction since most of us aren't just buying a "thing" but an article that carries all sorts of assurances and representations. We want to know that we have arrived at a place where we can have the luxury we want and probably deserve (if for no other reason than to compensate for the stresses of the very jobs that allow us to afford these things in the first place). With middle-class purses and upper-class desires, we have been swept swiftly along on a coursing current powered by women's economic growth, the flood tide of available credit, and a buoyant consumer culture that has figured out how to manufacture dreams and market them to us through neat, memorable brands.

BUT IT TURNS out these acquisitions have not delivered the happiness we expected. We may enjoy them for a moment, but then we move on to the next purchase, the next upgrade, the next "need" or necessary token of the dream. We do so in spite of the fact, as Juliet Schor points out, "that the psychological impact of all this materialism is pretty bad. There's a lot of evidence that depression, anxiety, stomach problems, and riskier behaviors are all correlated with higher levels of materialism." We continue to consume because we have come to believe that a dream life of love, comfort, and safety for ourselves or for our children can be obtained item by item.

I've come to think of women—like me—who rely on this promise we think money delivers to re-create all the safety and surety and identity of the mythic middle class as members of an *emotional* middle class. We don't spend simply to satisfy straightforward material needs or desires. Instead, our relationship with money is part of a more complex set of emotional expectations. Our actual and desired lifestyles are no longer bound by our economic abilities. Indeed, consumption has become untethered to class. According to an article in the *New York Times* about class in America, changes in production have enabled "factories in China and elsewhere [to] churn out picture-taking cell-phones and other luxuries that are now affordable to almost everyone." Furthermore, because of the changes in the ways in which credit is now extended, more people have more credit (and hence more debt) than ever before in history. The *Times* also reports that banks are more confident about measuring risk and "now extend credit to low-income families so owning a home or driving a new car is no longer evidence that someone is middle class."[5] All this has unleashed our appetites. We may be handcuffed to our paychecks, but the rise in standards of living and the easy access to goods that once were considered luxury items have blurred the lines between classes when it comes to what we think is our due as the heirs to the wealthiest, most prosperous nation in the world. Somehow, out of all this bounty, a muted sense of entitlement became our birthright. It has become possible to live in the style of the wealthy on a modest income.

A subtle shift has occurred. Desiring, achieving, or maintaining a lifestyle is now as much about self-fulfillment, pleasure, security, and individual identity as it is about the four traditional elements that define class distinctions: education, income, occupation, and wealth. As this new class consumes in order to satisfy more emotional needs or to create an emotional safe haven with material possessions, its members become trapped in a no-man's-land between need and want, trying to narrow the gap between the two.

Money doesn't define this emotional middle class as

much as the opposing forces of appetite and fear. We work hard to satisfy our desires, but we do so at the expense of grinding anxiety that comes from overextending ourselves financially. But because we are simultaneously aware of our privilege, we also feel guilty about what we have. Even as we yearn, we feel the moral tug of feeling like we shouldn't care about "things" so much. "I speak to women all the time who feel resentful if they don't have what they want, but then they feel guilty for the desires themselves," says Chellie Campbell, the author of *The Wealthy Spirit*. Campbell refers to herself as a "financial stress reducer"—not an investment counselor but someone who deals with women's emotional stress around money issues. "The characteristics of a member of the emotional middle class," she explains, "would be somebody who feels she still needs to strive to make ends meet but who has a lot of nice things so she feels she can't really complain too much."

This emotional middle class spans the generations. "I think younger people are more comfortable with their material side," observes Jean Chatzky, the financial editor of NBC's *Today* show. "Because they get credit at such an early age, to them, it's not even real. They are targets of tremendous marketing that creates expectations. But when you put all those micromessages we are getting from the marketers together, what they make you want is this perfect life. In order to have it, you need to have the big house and two cars and all those things that the middle class has locked itself into spending all of its disposable income on. The magazines and the TV shows all portray a much more affluent life than any real middle-class person can afford."

But in a world where "$200,000 is the new $100,000" (as the *New York Times* pithily pronounced), this emotional middle class is less an economic bracket than a state of mind—one that leads us to conduct our financial lives more by our feelings and fears than by our financial facts. We shop compulsively or in binges, building up credit card debt because we experience our desires as *needs*. We want the best for our children, so we overextend ourselves when it comes to buying homes in good school districts. We're now at the point where three-quarters of our after-tax incomes go to the fixed costs of mortgage, health insurance, child care, and taxes. (In the early 1970s, these costs represented about half of a middle-class family's income.)[6] Whatever our means, our fears and fantasies push us to our limits and beyond.

Indeed, no exact amount of money defines this group. I've talked to women who make $30,000 a year and women who pull in $300,000 annually who feel equally hungry and equally insecure. How much money we have or make may contribute to our sense of identity, but it's not the centerpiece. Those of us who are members of this class serve two gods: one that helps us make enough money to buy a home in a safe neighborhood with decent schools that don't require metal detectors at the door, and the other that disdains materialism and knows that friends and family and quality of life are greater than any assets we could have in the bank.

What is at stake for this emotional middle class? What are we so afraid of losing? It's not very dramatic or complicated, as it turns out. We want the safe and secure life of the halcyon middle class, even if the price tag on that life escalates every day. Yet instead of finding satisfaction with that life, we've come to venerate and imitate the very rich (whose lives are held out in front of us at every turn of the television channel or flip of the magazine page), even as we know that we could be the next ones to lose our jobs and have to take new positions paying half of what we made before.

This state of being has such real gravity that it affects all our behaviors with money. In order to stay within the safe confines of this emotional middle class, we will go into debt, spend on impulse, and lie awake for hours tossing about in regret. We will save too little, underinsure ourselves—all in the name of staying within the familiar and expected. Indeed, the pull is so strong that paradoxically, we spend on luxuries we can't afford and simultaneously deprive ourselves of real necessities. I've met more than one woman who had invested more heavily in her wardrobe and home than in her IRA and savings.

These fears and desires are so strong that women will often lie about their money habits rather than change them. When I tell Marty, a smart-looking woman in her early forties, about how I stole money from my husband, she laughs. "Oh, I've done that. I grew up with the women in my family peeling price tags off the expensive ice cream, sneaking money out of their husbands' wallets at night. One of my aunts who is married to my rich uncle is paying off her credit cards by taking $200 a night out of his back pocket as he sleeps off his scotch. He won't give her money directly, and she doesn't have access to her own accounts. But with several thousand in pocket change, he never misses the money." Marty goes on to tell me that she never tells her husband the truth about what she spends. She doesn't want the scrutiny and criticism.

According to a *Redbook–Smart Money* magazine survey, 40 percent of us still admit to lying to our partners about what something costs.[7] "I love to eat out and try all the newest hot spots," said one respondent. "But my husband hates to spend a lot on fancy restaurant meals. He just can't understand why anyone would pay $100 for a dinner for two. So when I go out with my girlfriends, I pay in cash and tell him I only spent $20." Rather than fight about different spending styles and priorities, many women will simply choose to tell a little white lie about what we spend.

Cindy, a cheerful brunette in her early forties, told me one of my favorite stories. After standing in a long holiday line at a Borders bookstore, she finally made it to the counter with her books and tapes. "Please charge these," she said, handing over the four most expensive purchases. "I'll pay cash for the rest." One woman standing behind her made a snorting sound. "What?" Cindy snapped. "Like you always tell what you spend? My husband freaks out over the credit card bills but doesn't blink at the cash I use, so why not get what I want and keep the peace? These are for him, anyway." The snorting woman smiled. Then every woman waiting in the line smiled. "You know what?" Cindy told me. "As my books were being gift wrapped, I watched almost every woman in line do exactly what I had done."

If we aren't in serious debt and we fudge the price of a dinner or the cost of a few books in order to do what we want, it's rarely enough to end a relationship or a marriage. But when it becomes systematic, when we aren't honest with ourselves about our inability or lack of desire to stop spending when we don't have the money, things can really explode. This was the case for Karen and her husband, Hank. During a few good stock market years in the late 1990s, they'd extended themselves financially. They invested in a nice house in a desirable suburb, put their two kids in a very prestigious private nursery school, and purchased a condominium at a popular ski resort. Then the market crashed. Hank, who had been managing the money, told Karen that she had to cut back. Sure, she said. What really happened was she began hiding her spending and bad-mouthing Hank.

Karen felt she could spend as much as she liked, since she'd been the one earning most of the money for the last fifteen years. While Hank worked as a stockbroker on commission, she'd been making a really nice living selling ads for a magazine publisher. Her job came with an expense account that she used freely for both lunches and dinners since she worked long hours and conducted her business over meals. This left her with money to lavish on herself, her family, and friends. "I love sending a friend beautiful flowers for her birthday, or giving my kids the latest 'thing' that's hot," she told me. "And I can't pass up beautiful clothes. Scarves, shoes, bags. If shoes were dollars, I could retire."

But within six months of the market downturn, Karen's employer went out of business, a delayed casualty of the dot-com bust, and she found herself out of a job with a six-month severance package that arrived in one check a few weeks after her dismissal.

"I once made this rule about what I would do when I had a windfall. I wouldn't spend it on one particular thing I wanted. Instead, I would put it in my bank account and not worry about money for a while," she said. "In my plan, I would divide it into thirds: a third for debt, a third for spending, and a third for saving."

Somehow that plan never came to fruition. Instead, Karen decided to treat herself to some time off. ("I *deserve* this," she rationalized.) For the first couple of months, she didn't put any money away. She kept the babysitter but took the kids to school trips, shopped, went to the gym, and had lunch with friends. She loved her life. At the end of six months, she had blown through the entire severance. She also had no desire to go back to work.

She figured that if she lived frugally, she could make her savings last so she wouldn't have to return to the work world. But instead of cutting back, she took up creative account-ing. "I told myself that if we just didn't go on a big vacation or redo the living room or go out as much, it would be okay for me to stay home for a while longer. I figured we could stretch the money out." But Karen found that changing her spending habits was harder than she thought. Every time she started to put the brakes on, she rebelled. She didn't stop sending flowers to her friends. She'd see an expensive shirt that looked good on her, and justified its purchase by saying she would buy fewer clothes, just better quality. She let the babysitter go but still went skiing with the family. She started fighting with Hank about how little money he was earning. Finally, unwilling to lower her standard of living further, she raided her 401(k) retirement account. Within eighteen months, fifteen years of savings were gone.

"I have this deprivation thing," she confessed. "It's like a starvation diet. When I go on one, I end up gaining weight because I get so mad that I can't eat. But really, I thought I would have more control over my spending. I didn't go nuts or anything, but I couldn't stop living the way I always had. Every time I cut back, I felt so deprived. No, not deprived—punished."

Karen knew her behavior made no sense. It was causing big trouble in her marriage. Hank couldn't understand why she couldn't discipline herself. She couldn't understand why he wouldn't get a better job. The fights looked like they were about money, but they were really about loss of power, lack of trust, and the basic fact that Karen didn't respect Hank, and at a certain level he knew it.

Karen couldn't give up her lifestyle. Without a beautiful home, without treats for the kids, she felt she was giving up her very self. What she didn't realize at the time was how unsafe she felt about Hank being the provider—something she'd avoided looking at as long as she had enough money to live as she wished regardless of his income. Having worked all her life to become a member of the emotional middle class, she couldn't pull back. "I had made money before; I figured it would come back. I didn't realize I wouldn't be able to get a grip. My sisters also have this money thing. One is obsessed with older rich men, and the other has no life. All she does is work, work, work because she's so afraid there will never be enough to live."

Karen and Hank ended up in marriage counseling. To pay for it, they rented their second home. (Hank wanted to sell it, but Karen managed to convince him it was an investment so he held on to it.) Their older child attended the local public school instead of the fancier private one where most of her friends went after nursery school. But Karen remains caught between deprivation and abundance, dependence and independence, responsibility and denial, still hoping that the money she and her husband need in order to regain their old lifestyle will magically reappear.

"I'M LIKE ONE of those battleships that sails just the slightest bit off course," Kerry, a single mother of ten-year-old Laurie, tells me as she settles in on the couch with a glass of wine. "Each month I spend just a little more than I have and sooner or later, I'm so far from where I think I'm going, there's no going back." She recently bought a condominium in Boston that, even as an attorney, she categorically cannot afford. But she says she couldn't bear living in her depressing old apartment anymore. "The T went by and rattled the windows a thousand times a day. I thought I'd go nuts."

At the age of forty-five, Kerry fears she's lost touch with reality. "I think it happened when I decided to have this kid on my own," she says with a sigh. "I told my boyfriend that I was too old not to have this child, and he said he didn't want to be a father. He told me, 'Choose one of us.' And that was that." So, with minimal child support, Kerry and her daughter live a comfortable life, but one that's on borrowed money and time.

Kerry has always worked. She became a lawyer not just for the money but because she wanted a better life than what she'd had during her hand-me-down childhood. By the time Kerry was born—she's the youngest of seven siblings—her parents didn't have much money, time, or energy left for her. "But I was told I could be anything I wanted to be. That turned out to be a lie, but I believed it then. But still, my mother made sure I made it to college."

"I feel like it's been one big bait and switch," she says bitterly. "Some life. I need so much cash each month to pay my mortgage, car payments, and credit card bills that I can't even take advantage of my company-matched 401(k) plan. I thought that making the kind of money I'm making, I'd be in fat city. But I came out of school with all these college loans and debt, and it's like everything escalated. I got here"—she waves her arm around her tastefully furnished living room—"only to find out that 'here' wasn't what I thought it was going to be."

Kerry complains that she has put very little away for her retirement but can't imagine not taking a taxi to and from work every day. She feels entitled to some luxury in her life because it is so hard to be a single mother with a demanding career. She's stuck trying to give herself the life she thought someone else would give her. "I know I'm not supposed to admit this because it's not politically correct, but I really thought that there'd be someone there to take care of me. That I wouldn't have to do it all. I love to work and all, but I also wanted the husband, you know? My biggest fear is that I'm going to end up like my mother now that my father's dead. No money. Rent-controlled apartment. Poor. I can't believe I've done all this just to end up in the same place as her."

I don't want to tell Kerry that her chances look pretty good for a repeat performance. She has $40,000 in a retirement account. That puts her way ahead of the average woman but nowhere near where she needs to be in order to retire above the poverty line.[8] For her, spending has an emotional urgency. It's more important for her to feel nurtured and free from deprivation in the short run than to know she will be safe in later years. Just the act of saving each month would be a reminder to her that no one is coming to take care of her. Defiantly, she spends. She'd rather live nicely in the piece of the American dream to which she feels entitled and postpone paying the bill for it. Her spending has an element of whistling past the graveyard.

As I talked to women who identified with these behaviors, I started to see that something other than materialism lay underneath all these frenzied purchases. Karen, Kerry, and I weren't buying for the thrill of the purchase. We were trying to satisfy the hunger for a picture-perfect life where everything is safe and beautiful, and where our children can grow up protected and happy. Our identities as women are so wrapped up in fulfilling these dreams that we inadvertently mortgage our lives as we try to fulfill them.

WE ARE ALSO passing along our hungers to the next generation. In our desire to re-create for our children the feelings of safety, comfort, and opportunity of that mythic middle class of the American dream, we are continually reaching for a life that's increasingly unaffordable and unsustainable. As a financial education expert, Joline Godfrey has spent more than a decade working with families and kids, trying to get them to see beyond their surface financial behaviors. She has observed that we're raising a generation of children with high lifestyle aspirations but no concept of how to achieve them. "Parents—particularly middle- and upper-middle-class parents (although this is afflicting working-class families as well)—are so tired and so overwhelmed by the demands on their children by the culture for what to wear, what to drive, where to live, that it's almost in resignation that they fill these kids' ATM accounts and empty their wallets to them," she says.

"Their kids grow up thinking, 'Somebody else will support me. I don't have to worry about this.' The dark side of this is what we're seeing unfold now. I refer to this phenomenon as a subsidy of adult children. You see this in the 'boomerang' kids—the ones who are now moving back home because they want to maintain the lifestyles but can't afford to do it by just working a regular job. The culture tells kids about a dream lifestyle, and their parents are too tired to fight the culture—so they give in to it. Now we're dealing with the consequences of young people who are draining their parents to maintain a lifestyle at the expense of pursuing their own independence."

These attitudes are both more prevalent and troublesome in girls, according to Godfrey. "It is stunning how many girls still think they will marry well," she tells me with sadness in her voice. She fears that, as a culture, we are not making financial independence a central element in girls' sense of identity, which means that it becomes much easier for them to disconnect from financial responsibility. If that happens, Godfrey warns, not only will the structural inequalities in the workplace persist—the difference in what men and women earn and lower numbers of women in executive positions—but women will continue to find themselves in danger of arriving at poverty's doorstep later in life.

Godfrey knows parents offer financial support to their

children as a form of love, but she believes that ultimately we're not helping our kids in doing so. "A man once told me that he had just given his daughter a substantial amount of money because he wanted her to be financially independent. I looked at him and said, 'No, you don't understand; you just made her financially dependent!' It's a strange and cruel conundrum: The families who—in the most loving, well-intentioned ways—give their children the most are in fact undermining them. Subsidizing children removes any incentive to go out and exercise any of the muscles of independence, which they need to have to take care of themselves."

WHEN FULFILLING AN emotional need creates a financial reality, our feelings about money can get pretty contradictory and twisted. I filched my husband's cash to give him the picture of happiness—an American dream realized. Not my husband's dream, or even my own as an adult, but the dream that had its roots in my childhood. By the end of elementary school, I may have been having terrific difficulties with fractions, but I had already started to see that the world was divided among those who bought fancy things, those who couldn't, and those of us who lived somewhere in between. I understood by then that my father and I belonged in this middle class. I knew we were dwarfed by the tall hedges of privilege that I saw in magazines, in movies, and on television. I wanted what they had. Not the money itself but the life of the imagined families that ate dinner together at perfect tables in perfect kitchens that I supposed were bright and warm and filled with the aromas of cooking—scenes that lay locked away from my sight, safely behind the privet. Not until years later would I come to see that I'd jumped to the conclusion that money could purchase more than things, more than security. I had invested it with the power to buy a dreamlike life.

As I grew up, I brought that belief with me to every area in my life: my work, my love life, and my marriages. I believed money had an alchemy that would transform the mundane into a golden life. The only problem was that it wasn't true. By the time I discovered I was mistaken, however, I'd loaded so many hopes and expectations onto this falsity that I knew of no other path to my heart's desires. I'd granted money the power to deliver almost everything I wanted: the promise of a happy life, a comfortable life, and a life of belonging, identity, and respect. That's an awful lot to purchase with just plain cash. But I never challenged the belief that it could. Instead, unaware, I mortgaged my sense of security as I tried to purchase my dream of the perfect life.

Whether I knew it or not, I'd joined the emotional middle class.

· 3 ·

FAMILY MONEY

THE FIRST TIME MY FATHER THREATENED TO DISINHERIT me, it was because I had Chris Davies jammed in my bedroom closet. I never knew how my dad, who had returned prematurely from a business trip, figured out I had a boy over against his strict instructions. But barely had the front door slammed before he marched into my room and threw open the closet door, revealing a squatting, skinny, frightened tenth grader wedged between a pair of Frye boots and the wall.

After he dispatched Chris, I was called on the carpet and threatened with the worst punishment in my father's arsenal: disinheritance. He didn't mean it, of course. Not that time, and not the next or the time after that. But it is revealing that my father's idea of the absolute worst thing he could do to me would be to pull the financial rug out from under my feet. The one he had worked so lovingly and so diligently to put there in the first place.

While I doubt this incident did any permanent damage, it did contain the seeds of what would eventually blossom into my two main insecurities about money: It could be lost at any time, and having any at all was entirely conditional on good behavior. Since providing for me expressed my father's love, the threat of withholding his support packed a wallop equivalent to a fiscal and emotional cannonball. Even though this heavy artillery was reserved for only the direst transgressions, the message was clear: As long as I kept the metaphoric sophomores out of my closet, I would remain under the protective wing of my father's emotional and financial care. If I rebelled, I'd be on my own.

This carrot-and-stick approach worked—but not in the way he intended. As a controlling device on my immediate behavior, I'd have to give it a C–. After all, I was a kid, and what teenager doesn't live in the land of no consequences? But on a deeper, emotional level, the threat of financial excommunication became a vital governor. Without being aware I was doing so, I interpreted this episode to mean that my father's love and care had stopped being a given. Although he certainly didn't intend for it to happen, emotional and economic abandonment became intertwined.

My father's monetary approach also delivered another subtle and corrosive message—one that was equally unconscious. Behind his largesse lurked the shadow of my inability. I interpreted his concern as implying that I needed his or someone else's financial care because I lacked the ability to generate enough security for myself. Therefore, I had better do whatever it took to stay in someone's good graces. That resulting lack of financial self-confidence stubbornly and irrationally persisted in spite of decades of steady paychecks. It also acted as a silent navigator in my choices, keeping me attached to solvent—but inappropriate—men and making me reluctant to leave jobs that didn't pay me enough. The fear of my own inadequacy infused the need for a steady income with an urgency that extended far beyond a need to simply pay the bills.

Money and love and safety became all mixed up inside me. I came to believe that only an ample cash flow could keep the financial wolf—the one who was always at my emotional door—from storming in and devouring and destroying my connection to everything and everyone I loved. That's an awful lot to ask of a paycheck: to make it the only thing protecting me from absolute fiscal and emotional poverty.

"Much of women's uneasiness can be traced to their childhoods," the author Victoria Secunda has observed. Secunda emphasizes the importance of emotional connections to a woman's happiness. She believes that because women fear losing their parents' love, their approach to money later in life derives from whether or not their parents—particularly their fathers—were supportive and involved. When fathers are both, girls learn they can be both feminine and competent. "But when a father is an exacting and/or distant presence, his daughter may intuitively figure out that the price of Daddy's care is her own frailty." [1]

Here's the ultimate irony: My father was exacting precisely because he loved me. He felt his true inheritance would be a self-sufficient daughter. He didn't realize his approach yielded a by-product. Certainly not one even remotely involving *frailty,* which, to me, is a first cousin to *needy* and *vulnerable.* And those words most definitely didn't fit either how I saw myself or how I behaved. But in whatever weird way that black box of a psyche makes its own sense of the influences in our lives, I responded to my father's economic give-and-take by developing a compliant, people-pleasing personality that I perversely refer to as my Inner Stewardess.

My Inner Stewardess showed up one day, little round overnight bag in hand, shortly after I started my first job. My boss had just told someone that "his girl" (me) would take care of something, and I faced the choice of telling him I was nobody's "girl" or smiling sweetly, shutting up, and staying employed. The stewardess came to my rescue, gracefully attending to whatever the now forgotten need was. Since then, she's become an anachronistic economic survival mechanism, one that on rational days—when I'm in command of my life and checkbook—rather horrifies me. But during those panicky episodes when I feel the urgent need to stay connected to money at any cost, she pops out with her jaunty little hat and white gloves, tight navy blue A-line skirt, and nylon hose—all those encumbrances meant for others' pleasure at the expense of her own comfort.

I purposely refer to her by this outdated and absolutely sexist title to remind me (at least when I'm aware of her presence) that her advice should be avoided because it comes from, and belongs to, another time and place entirely. Her stereotypically "feminine" style is out of synch with the surface facts and ways of my life. She's like my economic appendix—without any biological purpose but still present and capable of absorbing poisons, only to release them back through me over time.

While her presence hasn't stopped me from aggressively pursuing a career or economic independence, she occasionally reaches into my life and urges me to do anything and everything in order to make people happy and avoid rocking any boats. She hasn't been entirely useless, either. Through her, I learned to please bosses. (Happy bosses make for security and promotions. Promotions make for better salaries.) I learned to please men. (Happy men meant potential husbands. Potential husbands meant potential economic security.)

She's so good that most of the time I don't even know she's there.

As we discussed this strange phantom, Louann Brizendine, the psychiatrist and author of *The Female Brain,* explained to me that something very ancient and forceful and primal underlies my almost involuntary drive to please. "This is about survival. When you feel like your means of existence is jeopardized, it triggers the fear system in your brain, which causes panic. This can actually be good for you in that it can prevent you from doing stupid things. But only up to a point. When the fears are over the top, it can impair your mental functioning. When you go beyond that threshold of fear, it becomes toxic to your ability to think clearly and make good decisions."

Brizendine pointed out that three hundred million years of brain development informs my Inner Stewardess and her drive to mollify. She reminded me that women are hard-wired for behaviors that are affiliative. "We try to please in order to stay attached to the source of food, safety, income, because being banished equals death. When our survival mechanisms are tripped, we will be supplicating, accommodating, offer our necks—we will do anything in order to stay attached."

Some people—like my friend Robin—find the whole concept of an Inner Stewardess simply bizarre. The money/love/fear/attachment dynamic doesn't play a role in her financial life. It's not how she handles things. Maybe she doesn't need such a strange survival skill because her parents were very consistent and clear about money while she was growing up. They didn't mix money and love. Instead they told her that they would pay for her and her sister to go to college, but that state schools were all they could afford. If the girls wanted more, they had to get scholarships, but they would have to be self-supporting upon graduating. If they wanted extra money, they would have to earn it. They were told that they shouldn't plan on inheriting anything because there would be nothing to inherit. "But I also knew my parents didn't have more to give," she says. "I don't know how a child of more affluent parents would feel about those limits."

Robin is the healthiest woman I know when it comes to her relationship with money. She's had periods of financial challenge, yet to her, that's all they were. She knew her parents loved her even if they couldn't provide handsomely for her, and financial limitations in no way hinted at emotional ones. A self-made success in the business world, Robin has survived two divorces that have cost her dearly both emotionally and financially. But she knows how to keep the two separate. She doesn't load emotional freight onto financial transactions. "I'm highly employable," she says. "I can always take care of what I need to. Money is money— nothing more, nothing less."

MONEY ELBOWS ITS way into all our families, standing there like a silent other parent as we grow up. Each of us comes away with a special inheritance of attitudes and behaviors. Some come away healthy; others end up a bit more twisted. Some are thankful, others resentful. Some replicate their families' attitudes toward money, some compensate for them, and others rebel. Some families talk openly about money, others fight openly about money, and still others are completely mute on the subject. Some parents use money as a way of controlling their kids' behaviors, others as a way of showing love; still others elevate its power to a religious level. Some families work together to preserve family wealth, and others are torn apart by money envy. There are as many different approaches to money as there are families, which results in as many spending styles as there are people.

In every family, though, there are Hoarders and Spenders (and in every relationship, regardless of each person's previous spending patterns, ultimately each partner will assume one of those roles), both of which are expressions of control and power. Someone grants; someone withholds. One parent maintains eternal vigilance; the other threatens stability. Variations on these two broad archetypes include Worriers and Dreamers, Strategic Shoppers (who contemplate their purchases and who feel increasingly nervous with each ring of the cash register) and Impulse Shoppers (who feel more euphoric with each purchase), the Bargain Hunters, Retail Shoppers, and the Switch Hitters (like me, who alternate among these styles in rapid succession depending on our moods). There are Stockpilers (who need tons of money to feel good about themselves) and Philanthropists (who either feel the need to share their good fortune or can't get rid of their guilt at having money until they give it away).

We often develop these modes of behavior in response to how our families treated money. As children, we watched and learned as we saw how money expressed love, stood for power, or created safety. As adults, each time we repeat their behaviors (even ones we don't like), we connect back to the familiar regardless of whether doing so brings feelings of safety or peril, love or loss. In this way, our families become the architects of our money lives. Christine, a forty-three-year-old woman I met through an online financial support group, remembers: "My father constantly worried about money. To him, that's how he showed us his love. My mother, on the other hand, was addicted to shopping. It was how she showed her love for my sister and me. She'd buy us tons of stuff. She would go to the mall and come home and hide the purchases. Then, when my dad was in a good mood, she'd show him about half the stuff."

Christine's parents divorced when she was in the eighth grade, but before they separated, they fought constantly and bitterly about money. "My father always accused my mother of being completely irresponsible. That she was hurting us, her daughters, because she was wasting all the money that would be ours one day," she says. "My mother never worked. Going shopping is what she did. My sister and I didn't complain because we got great stuff, but after a while we started to feel pretty guilty—like we were causing all the problems between our parents."

After the divorce, Christine and her sister moved with their mother from their suburban home to a small two-bedroom apartment. "My mom was furious with my father and complained all the time about how cheap he was. She wouldn't let us use the dryer because she said it ran up the electricity bill too much. She had to go to work, which she really hated. She constantly told us how rich he was and how poor we were, and whenever we would be with my dad, she made sure we went shopping," recalls Christine. "She was very bitter about her measly alimony and wanted to stick my father with as many bills as she could."

As an adult, Christine lives far from both parents. But even though she's distanced herself physically from her family's Hoard-and-Spend mentality, that seesaw dynamic turned out to be a comfortable emotional touchstone. She has re-created financial situations that trigger feelings about money that come directly from her childhood. "In spite of myself," she says, "I'm turning out to be so much like my mother. I have a chip on my shoulder that I think only money can satisfy. I reward myself with things I can't afford whenever I get down. It's my way of self-love. I hide what I buy from my husband because he yells at me. I especially hide my credit card bills. Some people have comfort food. I comfort-shop. Then, just to top it off, I beat myself up for being so bad with money. It's like I've taken the worst parts of both my parents."

The psychiatrist Gail Saltz refers to patterns of behaviors like Christine's as "stories" we tell ourselves that allow us to remain emotionally connected to our families. "Here's the dirty little secret," she says. "As children, our stories told us we could hold on to love and feel emotional order and safety if we acted in a certain way. But as adults, the opposite happens. The stories rob us." Christine created a money story to go back in time to resolve her feelings about her family, but instead, this story actually carries her problems forward into her mature life.

Althea, a forty-year-old marketing executive, traces her

ambivalence about her financial responsibilities directly back to her family. "Part of me secretly wanted to do what the other women in my family were doing: shopping, lunching, letting someone else bring home the bacon. I never admitted this to myself." Althea clearly saw the flip side of the equation: "No matter what anyone said," she recalls, "they were controlled by their husbands' money. A dance had to be done around every bill. A song was sung around every purchase. Terror accompanied every shopping trip. Grandmothers, aunts, younger cousins—it was always the same." At ten years old, Althea made a promise to herself: that she would always have her own money. "I hated the idea of being controlled, but in making that promise, I was totally unaware of the roiling conflict I set off in myself. So, for nineteen years, I have worked, not wanting to work and not wanting *not* to work. I was completely unaware of this."

Her unconscious conflict came to the surface incidentally. Her husband, a self-employed attorney, came home one night and announced he'd settled a big case that day. "Out of my mouth came, 'Good. We're one step closer to my being a housewife.' I laughed, but he knew better and turned a chalky white at the idea that I might quit working. He was happy being married to someone who could pay the bills."

Althea has never really resolved her mixed feelings about having to earn money. She's caught between wanting it and being repelled by what she saw in her family. "So I married someone who would make sure I had to keep working. Though I concentrate very hard when I pick Lotto numbers, somehow, I still have to make money. I guess that's not an accident."

Growing up, we watch the other women in our lives. We absorb their experience, and it shapes ours. Maryann, a thirty-two-year-old retail buyer, grew up in "financial chaos." Her father, a union autoworker, frequently found himself on picket lines and ultimately lost his job when his plant closed. He never got a well-paying job again and spent the rest of his life sporadically employed and bitter about what had happened. Maryann's mother became a nurse's aide, and the family lived on whatever they could scrape together. Her mother clearly resented their situation, and Maryann would cringe each time her mother would shrilly attack her father for any purchase he made.

At sixteen, Maryann, the oldest of four kids, went to work every day after school making deliveries for her local drugstore. "Everything I made went to the family. I still feel badly about it, but I just had to get out." At eighteen, Maryann got a scholarship and worked her way through Michigan State. She married her college sweetheart, who came from a financially stable family. "He was supposed to work in his father's mattress store," she recalls. "But these discounters came in, and within a couple of years they were out of business and Bobby wasn't trained for anything else. He would get a sales job and then just sort of let it all fall apart." Bobby developed a passion for computers and spent more and more time in the garage taking them apart and rebuilding them.

Maryann has found herself in her old role of financial supporter. But she refuses to allow herself to get "sucked dry like a vampire" as she felt her mother had been. So she created a separate savings account—one her husband couldn't access. She's afraid that Bobby, now her husband of ten years, will lose all their money if she doesn't hide some away. "I won't let Bobby near the bills. He'd blow everything we have on his toys. He never met a piece of electronics he didn't want. He has no sense of money." (When I ask Bobby if it bothers him that Maryann is in charge of the couple's finances, he says he doesn't mind since she makes most of the money. But he does resent the accusation that he's irresponsible. "It's her crazy family that never had any financial stability," he points out in his own defense. "She just can't trust anyone with money because growing up, she never knew what was going to happen. I love her, but she has some serious control issues that get dumped on money.")

Maryann resents that she has to be the one taking charge. She feels like no one will ever look out for her. And when she looks in the mirror, she increasingly recognizes her mother's disappointment as it carves lines in her face.

It doesn't matter if we rebel against, compensate for, or end up repeating our families' way with money. We can't run away from the fact that what we saw growing up can invisibly shape our own behaviors and emotions. Sometimes it can reveal itself in insignificant ways, as is the case with Justine, whose frugal mother hoarded everything. "To this day, every Baggie gets rinsed and used again. It drives me nuts. Particularly because now I can't throw one away without my mother's voice in my ear telling me that when I was the one making the money, I could be wasteful. I'm forty years old. I have a family of my own. I have plenty of money. But I still can't throw away a stupid plastic bag. And the worst thing is, my daughter is getting to be the same way. She can't part with anything and is obsessed with how much things cost."

But sometimes our reactions can carry tremendous import. As we try to avoid re-creating our parents' behavior with money, we can make inadvertent decisions that affect far more than our bank accounts. Eva's mother routinely pocketed money from her father's paycheck without telling anyone except Eva. "I watched her steal money from my dad so he wouldn't gamble it all away. He had a problem. No wonder I've never been able to trust anyone enough to get married," she says. "I will never trust anyone with my money. What if they lose it? Spend it? Who would take care of me?"

FROM MY EXTENDED family, I learned that money measured your worth: You were a success if you made lots of it (and success was very important); if you didn't, you fell down a few notches on the social food chain. My father grew up in the Depression. He rebelled against his more "artsy" father, who chose painting and teaching over the legal profession for which he'd been trained. Consequently, my father became the first in his family to escape the Upper

West Side of Manhattan for the suburbs. His parents had made it as far as Queens, where they lived in a ten-story red-brick building that looked like half of all the buildings in the borough. (His father would die there on the afternoon of my ninth birthday, propped up in the brown corduroy chair with the saggy ottoman when he was, instead, supposed to meet my father and me in Manhattan for a matinee performance of *Fiddler on the Roof*.) This, my father did not want for himself—and making a good living ensured he would avoid his father's fate.

My mother came from "a good family." After she died, much of my care came from my grandmother (who, an aunt once told me, had hinted that her daughter had married outside their social circle). Even as my grandmother sniped, my father's fortunes soon intersected hers, then eclipsed them. He, like many men who fought in World War II and who benefited from the GI Bill, enjoyed a rather straightforward march up the economic ladder.

My maternal grandparents, on the other hand, may have kept their preconceptions of right and wrong and their upper-crust prejudices, but their fortunes declined steadily every year. For most of my childhood, they lived elegantly in Philadelphia on Rittenhouse Square in an apartment whose sofas had sage-colored slipcovers that had to be changed seasonally. This grandfather would not die there. A series of strokes steadily reduced him from a once financially prominent man to one whose only form of communication was whistling. He starved himself to death in the old-age home where my grandmother, unable to cope, had deposited him. By then, most of their money was gone, and my grandmother lived in a series of smaller and smaller apartments that made her furniture seem larger and larger. Eventually, she, too, tried to kill herself. However, as with many things in her life, she was disappointed by her efforts. She succeeded only in being incarcerated in a nursing home that smelled of pine-scented disinfectant and which we seldom visited.

From my father, I inherited the belief that there was only one acceptable financial direction. Like rings on a tree, my money circle was supposed to enlarge each year. Each time I depart from that way of measuring my progress, it sets off an internal conflict. The conflict goes like this: I provide money, which means I love my family and will show it by taking care of them. But due to an inability to figure out how to pick my kids up from school and work at the same time, I decide to take a job that pays less but allows more flexibility. As I rocket back and forth between value systems and roles—traditional male, traditional female—everything starts to feel very all-or-nothing. I provide for my family, or I abandon my family. I feel safe or feel doomed—often in the same afternoon. No wonder I've often found work exhausting and anguishing. So much is at stake. I'm trying to live up to the financial expectations of my father's world and the maternal ones of my mother's. I accomplish neither to my satisfaction.

Sometimes it feels as if we can't escape our families' patterns. Sandra, a woman in her thirties, responded to her mother's helplessness by vowing that she would never depend on anyone for money. "I have this deprivation and abundance thing with money. Like I will always be wanting a little bit. My father was an artist; my mother worked at home. My older sister has an obsession with rich men, my younger one has always taken care of herself, but she's a workaholic. There's a lot of deprivation underneath all our behavior. I feel I have maxed out. I think about it, and I wonder why I always feel like I'm running."

Sandra went to Debtors Anonymous for a while not because she had bills she couldn't pay but because she didn't feel she had a sense of what "normal" responsible financial behavior was. "Spending had all this stuff attached to it," she says. "For me, it's similar to the food thing. I feel like I'm a good person if I don't eat too much, and if I'm out of control, there's some moral judgment for me. Like I'm not being a good steward of my life. I'm not treating myself with respect."

If being a bad steward were the only consequence of Sandra's feelings of abundance and deprivation from her childhood, it would have been fairly benign. But in her early thirties, Sandra met a man at a resort town in Massachusetts and fell in love. "I should have been tipped off when two weeks after I met Ted, he'd get up in the morning, stretch his arms, and say, 'I love the feeling of leaving the house with no money in my pocket and not spending all day.'" Ted was beyond broke. To Sandra, he had absolutely no interest or discipline or respect when it came to money. To him, it simply wasn't important. He'd come from a very wealthy family and had defended himself against their controlling ways by not caring about money at all.

Ten years and two children later, Sandra makes the money and Ted manages their home and family. But one day, Ted came home with a new bike. A $1,500 mountain bike, to be exact. Sandra's blood boiled. "Nice of him to be so free with my money," she said to herself. This thought was immediately followed by an attack of shame. "He's so frugal, I can't believe I even let that bother me," she tells me as her cheeks flush with shame. "But it really did. I still have this thing in my head that says there'll never be enough for all of us, never enough to go around or provide real long-term security. I bit off Ted's head for the bike, and it was all about the fact that I felt it would deny *me* something. I can't afford to put that kind of stuff on my marriage. We just had the hugest fight about it. And why? Because it felt like a flashback to my parents. I do not want to be them, but there it was. It all felt so familiar. When my dad would get a little money, if my mother spent it on something he thought was frivolous, we'd hear about it for days. We'd all cringe, knowing she would get back at him by making him feel as small as he possibly could about the fact he so seldom brought home any money."

In spite of herself, Sandra found that she continued to make Ted feel guilty about the bike. She couldn't let it go. Every day she'd make another little dig at him until he finally exploded, informing her that if she was trying "to cut his balls off," she was doing an excellent job. Sandra felt terrible because she knew it was true. "I was acting just like my mother, using the only thing that had worked effectively on Dad: accusing him of not being a man because he couldn't provide. It was ugly." Sandra admits that when she feels any threat to her money, she can get pretty savage since it brings up all the turmoil from her childhood. "It feels really urgent—like a matter of life and death," she says. "Even though I know intellectually that's not true, it still feels that way."

While Sandra lashes out when she's insecure about money—money gives her the power to do that, she feels— Stephanie has a completely different reaction when she gets anxious: She placates anyone who has the ability to dispense money. She goes underground and behaves indirectly. "My mother was a doormat," she tells me, sounding disappointed. "She had to beg my father for money for us to go shopping. She would make me put on a fashion show afterward so that my father would feel his money went to good use. It was humiliating. She had to account for every penny."

Stephanie's biggest regret about herself is that she's an "underearner." "I'm not broke because I spend a lot," she admits, "but I'm afraid to ask for a raise because what if they fire me? What if they think I'm greedy? I just don't feel I can risk it."

As an attorney, Gretchen makes more money than her husband. A lot more—something foreign to Gretchen's mother. "You're too tough on Will," Gretchen's mom scolds her about her husband. "You have to let him control the money, or he won't feel like a man, and that will cause problems. Besides, you're good at making money, not managing it." Gretchen tries to explain that she and Will have put their money together and make joint decisions. But Gretchen admits that sometimes she doesn't see Will as someone she can rely on to make good financial decisions because he's so laissez-faire about money. "I try not to let him see I feel this way," she says. "But the other day, when we were told we basically had to rip out our front steps and rebuild them because they were unsafe, I realized that I was cutting Will off in the conversation with the contractor because I didn't trust his money judgment. We had a fight later that night, one of our big ones, and I know that I was partly fighting with my mother because all I could hear was her saying, 'Be a lady, let him handle it,' and all I could think was, 'I'm the one who cares about money in this relationship!'"

Gretchen has got her own version of the Inner Stewardess, one that may sound like her mother but now is part of her. "Sometimes I let Will make decisions about our IRA or something because I don't want to undermine him. I think I do that as kind of a fantasy because it makes me feel taken care of—kind of like he's my dad, someone who will make sure I won't run out of money. I like it when he pays for dinner. I like not having to carry a wallet. I know it's sounds silly, but it feels good. But then when it comes to investments and stuff, I get all edgy about his decisions and second-guess him, and it can end pretty badly. Not a good strategy."

Gretchen wrestles with her mother's version of femininity and money. Like many women in her generation, she leads a much more complex financial life than her mother did. Her mother worked as a librarian but had no qualms about being dependent. She expected this, so it was not at odds with her identity. But Gretchen, at this point, leads a more conventional "male" financial life—one that closely resembles her father's. And during the course of her life, she might inhabit any one of three roles: her current role as the sole or principal provider, the more traditional female dependent model, or somewhere in between. Few women embody only one role or another. More likely, we will alternate among all three at various points in our lives. But each role takes an emotional bite out of the other options not taken.

OUR ATTEMPTS AT reconciling these conflicting identities create a weird state of being where we feel that no matter what we do, we're not right. If we love our kids, should we provide for them or stay home with them? If we aren't married, is it because we're too economically independent to attract a husband? Do men think we need them less? We look around and see different women who've made different choices with different economic consequences. We see one woman who creates her own financial security living right next to a woman who depends on her husband for all her money. This creates an unhealthy dance of envy, superiority, and judgment. "Wait until those soccer moms get dumped for a younger version of themselves," one woman tells me with an edge of bitterness in her voice. "She's just abandoned her kids for her career," another woman says, assailing someone she regards as a friend. "It's so selfish. Why bother having kids if all you're going to do is turn them over to a nanny and work?" The antagonisms may express themselves outwardly toward other women, but the battles rage within ourselves, making the emotional ambivalence about money even more painful.

These dueling roles have often been referred to as "the Mommy Wars," but that label can distract us from the fact that what's at stake isn't simply how we raise our children. Turning one mother's path against another's diminishes the fact that huge economic pitfalls exist for women as economic entities. Because our culture still doesn't place economics at the core of a girl's identity (as it does with boys), girls grow up in families that don't stress the economic consequences of mothering decisions. Yet they are profound. In her groundbreaking book *The Price of Motherhood,* the Pulitzer Prize–winning journalist Ann Crittenden points out that when a woman leaves the workplace to raise her children, she does so at the expense of her long-term economic security. Inflexible workplaces, which still work best for single men or men with wives at home, guarantee that women will have to cut back—if not quit their jobs entirely—once they become mothers. Besides the lost wages (which Crittenden estimates to be close to $1 million over the working life of a college-educated woman),[2] pensions don't get funded, social security is diminished or jeopardized, and, in the case of divorce, the principal care-taking spouse invariably is left worse off financially than the one who has worked without interruption.[3]

"Women don't consider the economics when they start a family," she says to me when we discuss this topic. "However, that's not an excuse for taking economic advantage of a woman's feelings. To do so is unconscionable. But that's what happens. People are made to pay to love and care for their children."

Yet, as she points out, we're dealing with an almost primordial force. "There is hardly a soul in the world who doesn't want a child or a pet to love and take care of. The biological desire to have and nurture children is a fundamental human quality." As is the need for economic survival. Thus a huge part of the Mommy Wars lies not only in the conflict of roles, identities, even ways of valuing ourselves, but in an intractable standoff between two biological imperatives: the need to love and reproduce and the need to have an income.

There are few, if any, family histories in which these opposing forces are resolved. No previous generations have successfully managed to combine the economic and nurturing worlds of our fathers and mothers. We're left alone to cobble together our private, individual solutions. But we do this at our peril, warns Crittenden. "For women, a big part of our culture is that feeling that everything that happens to them is their fault. They feel they have to solve this issue by themselves since they got themselves into the problem in the first place." Crittenden believes that younger women are especially vulnerable to these feelings because they think there are no more "women's" problems—that the revolution has been fought and won—a belief that leaves them feeling that such problems are now their fault. "This thinking is insidious and prevents social change. As long as women perceive their situations to be due to their own shortcomings, nothing will change. The younger women especially don't know what's hit them. All of a sudden, they are losing a million dollars in lifetime earnings, or they suddenly divorce and have vastly compromised lives." Unlike women in previous generations who were more economically dependent, today's women are stunned to discover an amazing gap in our discussion of our finances. "Nobody tells women what to expect, so they aren't prepared," says Crittenden. "They aren't prepared for the ground rules of marriage, motherhood, or divorce. They think they're in a partnership and everything is equal and therefore equal financially. And it's not true."

In her talks around the country, Crittenden tries to convey to women that their situations aren't the result of their individual failures or even their own family issues, but instead are part of a systematic and structural problem. "I tell them, 'Listen, if you break your leg, it's a personal problem. But if you have an economic problem that millions of other people have, then you don't have a personal problem; you have an economic and social problem.'"

Until we see the *cost* of motherhood and add that information to our *experience* of motherhood (both our mothers' and our own), we will continue to face only a part of the motherhood/work issue. We will continue to live with two sets of examples and instructions—one from our mothers and one from our fathers—neither of which can possibly be followed completely. These two sets of examples, two sets of values, and two intractable and mutually exclusive economic systems leave us riddled with confusion, anxiety, and a lingering sense of failure.

These past few decades of rapidly changing role models have taken their toll. As Beth, a thirty-year-old single woman, says, "We can't win. One day there's a cover story in *New York* magazine about women who make more than their husbands, and the next week the *New York Times Magazine* is extolling the lives of stay-at-home moms. None of our role models have held up. No wonder young women are so torn about what they're supposed to do about making money." In trying to embrace all financial roles, we often feel we've done none of them well. We've seen our mothers go from homemakers to executives. We've praised them and damned them for their choices. We've followed their examples and rebelled against them. But their experiences are cut from the cloth of another time and place. When we adopt the mantles of motherhood and economic provider, there may be no easy or individual solutions. But there are huge economic consequences.

· · ·

OUR ULTIMATE FAMILY legacy is one of mixed messages. Women, trying to fulfill both traditional parental roles, inherit frustration at trying to fulfill incompatible imperatives. We inherit confusion about whether we're supposed to be stereotypically feminine or masculine, whether we are going to be dependent or independent. Along with our families' spending styles, prejudices, and values, we try—through trial and error—to learn from our own mistakes and those of others.

At times, there is some clarity. Shelley is twenty-nine and still stinging from having broken up with her boyfriend, Noah. "I thought this was going to be it. I really thought he was the one, partly because he made me trust him. He was kind of grown up about money and investments, and I liked that." But it turned out Shelley had a very different set of financial behaviors and beliefs than Noah did. "He was so totally dependent on his parents, particularly his mother, emotionally and financially. She couldn't handle it when we started dating seriously. She couldn't accept him making independent decisions with me."

The other nail in the relationship coffin, Shelley tells me, was that Noah wanted a traditional marriage, in which she would stay home and raise the kids. "Even though, growing up, I would say I wanted to stay home for part of my kids' childhoods, at the same time I didn't want to do what my mother did mostly because of the consciousness that women like her realize at a certain age that they don't have any skills. That's a scary place to be."

Shelley tells me that the message the women of her

generation got from watching their mothers was that they should choose to do something they value beyond net worth. "My friends and I saw that you can't have it all, so you should do something that matters to you. You can have a lot of things in your life—career, work, family—but you cannot have them work at the same time and have them work well. Your marriage will suffer, or your finances will suffer, or your kids will suffer, or you will suffer." Shelley has concluded that since she can't have everything, she wants to make sure she's happy with what she does have. "If you invest in your kids or marriage, one day those people may grow up or wake up and not want the same things you want for them. If you invest your life into making money, one day you can find yourself out of a job with nothing else to hold on to. My parents taught me that by their experiences, and I swore I would never be like that."

But instead of economic freedom, Shelley is dealing with something that many younger women face: the prospect of a more extended dependence on her parents. "I'm trying to be my own person, but I still need my parents to bail me out," she confesses. She had given up her apartment, furniture, and many of her possessions when she moved in with her boyfriend. When they broke up, she went into debt starting all over again in a new home. "I'm the Target and Ikea queen," she says, attempting a chuckle. "I hate to ask my parents. I always knew they would be there for me as backup. Not as rescuers, but just there if I really needed them. But I'm not comfortable asking. What happens is that my dad calls and asks, 'How're you doing for money?' And I tell him, 'Well, I'm kind of strapped, but I'm doing okay.' And a month later, it's almost like I've reverted to this weird kid thing. He'll send me a check with a comment like, 'Don't say anything to Mom.' He's not trying to control me; it's just his way of telling me he loves me. But it's really ironic because every time he does that, he sends me the message that I can't take care of myself. And look at me. He's right. It's also weird that he does it with money because that's what broke up my relationship."

For many of Shelley's friends, the financial strings stretch across the generations. "Even though they've got a couple of kids of their own, their parents are so enmeshed in their finances," she says. "It's kind of infantilizing and undermining. Like they can't make any big financial moves on their own because what if they do it wrong?"

This may be the final legacy of families and money. In their attempts to make us safe, and to show us they love us, our parents inadvertently created a legacy of insecurity about our ability to take care of ourselves. Even as we live our lives as adult women, some of us still remain financial children so we can stay attached to those whose control, if not financial largesse, makes us feel loved and secure.

· 4 ·

WORKING GIRL

I ROCKETED OUT OF COLLEGE WITH A DEATH GRIP ON the bottom rung of the career ladder. I was ambitious, hopeful, idealistic, and energetic. I was going to get rich, change the world, and be a success. I didn't exactly know how I was going to do all these things, but I figured I'd find some way. "Go into advertising," my father said (panicked, no doubt, that he'd otherwise end up supporting his liberal arts daughter until someone else came along). "You'll do great!" Being all of twenty-one years old and somewhat of a know-it-all, I proclaimed that I wanted to do something with my life that was more elevated than selling Tampax or foot powder. Money, I sniffed, was less important than meaning.

My very first paycheck—in the princely amount of $85—came from my job working at a public access cable television station with the grandiose title of production assistant. What I really did was fetch coffee and props and occasionally plug in something. My favorite show was *I Can Do Anything with Fran Beck,* and she meant it; the program was vaguely pornographic and featured Fran and anyone else who wanted to "do" something with her. That didn't turn out to be the career starter I'd envisioned, though, and it was soon followed by my first "real" job, which I found through that time-honored search engine—the Yellow Pages. It was under *C* for Canfield Press. (There had been no openings in any of the *A*'s or *B*'s.)

The job paid $6,500 a year.

My interview consisted of a typing test and a rather harried woman asking me if I dealt well with high-maintenance individuals. Given my inability to type with either speed or accuracy, I figured I'd better pass myself off as an expert in whatever a high-maintenance individual was. She hired me on the spot as an editorial assistant. (In retrospect, I think my chief qualifications were that I was breathing and had showed up for the interview.)

A few weeks earlier I had moved to San Francisco, where I was cohabiting with three guys (one of whom was my boyfriend, naturally) in a small flat in the Mission District, one house in and one story up from what turned out to be the major shopping corner for transsexual prostitutes. I was absolutely flat-busted broke, and my roommates weren't much better off. Rick was an elfin man who only wore tie-dye and was getting his Ph.D. in the science of mushrooms, which he grew under the sink in our only bathroom. My boyfriend was an idealistic Vista volunteer who made half of what I did (we survived, in part, on his food stamps), and the third roommate was an enthusiastic Marxist organizer named Andrew who greeted me every morning with a booming, "Hail, Comrade."

My work involved typing and filing and covering for a textbook editor who had trouble finding his way into the office every day. Maybe I wasn't editing the next *War and Peace,* but it wasn't a widget factory either. My boss was a flaky guy with a shaky grip on reality—one that finally eluded him altogether when he had some kind of break-down and never made it back into the office, leaving behind me and a bunch of Valium spilled in a desk drawer.

Nine months into the job, the president of the company came out from New York to visit and glad-hand the natives. With the best of intentions, he asked all the impoverished assistants about our career hopes. "I certainly don't want to be an editor," I exclaimed. "I'm broke. There has to be something that pays better than this." It hadn't taken long for reality to put its first scratch on the shiny new coat of my principles. Impressed by my response (it was almost the 1980s, and any signs of greed were viewed as indications of healthy ambition), he offered to see what he could do for me if I ever came back East.

Three months later, after depositing the idealistic boyfriend in law school and fleeing my impoverished San Francisco existence and the Marxist mushroom roommates, I showed up at his office door in New York City. "I want to understand the business side of publishing," I announced. It seemed everyone around me was going to law school or business school, and while I had no interest in ever darkening another academic door, I figured they might be on to something and that if I ever wanted to make a decent living, I better have some "hard" skills. He got me a job working for the chain-smoking, nail-biting director of strategic planning, where I spent my days totaling columns of profit-and-loss statements at the stratospheric salary of $16,000 a year. There were no personal computers in 1978, and everything I did involved an adding machine and a succession of pencils. I could never get the columns to foot properly. Once I erased a summary sheet so many times I had to glue a little piece of paper behind the original.

It had taken a little more than a year for me to substitute the search for meaningful work with the search for meaningful money. It was a horse trade I would be making in one form or another for the rest of my career. What I didn't know then, but would eventually discover, was that the trade involved much more than I thought. In time, who I thought I was and what I thought I believed would end up on a collision course. Was I going to work to live or live to work? How important was it to make money, and what was I willing to trade away for security? These big questions would sneak up on me buried inside salary negotiations, maternity leaves, and internal debates over just how far I was willing to go along to get along.

. . .

BUT NONE OF these looming conflicts was apparent in the beginning. In fact, when you've never made anything more than babysitting money, those first paychecks are a miracle. You work, you get paid. As Maureen, a willowy thirty-three-year-old Internet producer, recalls: "No one could tell me what to do anymore. I was free. When I got out of college, work was where I met people, and it was a way to pay the bills. I didn't take what I did very seriously; my life was so much more important. I shared an apartment with three other girls. We took our checks, cashed them, bought clothes, and went to bars. If you opened our refrigerator, it was a museum of old doggy bags. I don't think I went grocery shopping once. I took a job as an assistant to this guy, and we worked and worked, and I kept getting promoted, and all of a sudden, I had stock options and a nice salary. It's that old thing—when you've got nothing to lose, you've got nothing to lose. But when I had something to lose, I started to get stressed about things. Office politics. Job insecurity. You know, stuff."

The first time I realized that "stuff" was getting to me was five years into my publishing career. I'd quit that numbers-crunching job and started my career all over yet again, this time as an assistant to the associate publisher of the trade-book division of the same company. Even though I'd had to cut my salary, I figured it was worth it to be working with real books, ones I actually wanted to read.

I was madly in love with what I did and felt I'd found my true calling. (I still couldn't type, but one of my performance appraisals filed away in a warehouse somewhere has the commendation that I "gave great phone.") The 1980s had dawned, and publishing—as unprofitable as it can be—was not immune to threats of takeovers. In order to thwart potential unwelcome suitors, many companies, including the one I worked for, reorganized, pared down, and began laying off staff in what would become, over the next twenty years, a torturous version of corporate anorexia.

One morning before work, my boss and mentor—to whom I was utterly devoted—called me at home. It was so early that I took the phone into the bathroom and sat on the mat by the toilet because my new boyfriend was still sleeping. "I'm quitting," he announced. "They want me to make headcount cuts I don't feel are right. I told them to take my salary and save a couple of positions." I couldn't believe it. How could the company let him do that? They knew how brilliant he was; they knew how good he'd been for the company. How could they let him leave? I cried for two days, mourning the loss of both my beloved mentor and my naive illusion that employers cared about their employees.

Without knowing it, somewhere in those early years, I'd struck a one-sided bargain with my work that had just been violated. I agreed to give my employer long hours, all my best thinking and hardest work in exchange for an opportunity to contribute and have those contributions rewarded with job security and recognition. Neither of those two things involved money—directly.

In my twenties, I wasn't thinking about my salary too

much since I assumed it would inevitably reflect fair compensation for work well done. At that age, I was immortal. I had plenty of time to make money. And I innocently trusted that there was a sort of universal fairness doctrine that treated money as a quid pro quo—that if I performed well, I would be paid in kind. Instead, I focused on the recognition—the weird pass-along of praise and advancement—I seemed to require in order to form my sense of who I was and to prove (mostly to myself) that what I did mattered to myself and to others. Without knowing it, I had transferred a fundamental need for recognition from my personal life to my professional one. In doing so, I was now emotionally beholden to a corporation, looking for it to provide me with the mix of money and meaning I needed in my life. As long as I loved my work and kept marching up the hierarchy, this dependency didn't bother me. Indeed, I was content with single-digit annual salary increases because I loved what I did.

But as I sat in my bathroom on that October morning and listened to my boss's news, that contract was torn to pieces. Suddenly, this whole work-and-reward thing wasn't delivering what I thought it promised. Meaningful work alone couldn't compensate for the betrayal I felt. It was time to take a new look at the agreement I'd made. I dragged myself into work that day only to find that my mentor's stand hadn't made a difference: The company had fired everyone on the list anyway. And even though I followed him out the door a month or so later (he'd gotten a new job and had hired me immediately), I now went to work each morning armed with the jaded understanding that good work alone didn't guarantee anything. We were all expendable.

So, in a strange twist, I did what many women I spoke with often do. I changed from a fearless young tiger to a more indirect and political animal. I downplayed the more outwardly "male" behavior, in my case, hiding it under the cute-little-kid-sister act. (Some women admit they played up the traditionally female and somewhat sexy approach. Virginia, a sales representative for a television network, quips, "I took off the business suit and put on the push-up bra.") I muted my outspokenness even when I disagreed with those above me on the food chain, and I also minimized my salary demands. I decided I would be supportive and silent and somewhat self-effacing when it came to coworkers, bosses, and money. If I didn't demand, they'd be more apt to like me and less inclined to fire me. Every time I started to open my mouth to ask for more, my Inner Stewardess would tell me to close it. "Quiet," she'd command. "You don't want to get fired, and if you start getting pushy, they will see you as a problem." She seemed to show up at every annual performance appraisal. Instead of "Gee, Matthew is making $10,000 more than I am for the same job," I found myself saying, "Thank you. Thank you so very much."

Increasingly, I learned to twist myself every which way simply to hold on to what I had. Financial need clearly accounted for some of that emotional glue. But a great deal also came from the fact that as the years went by, much of my identity derived from my work. I wasn't married, and I had little else in my life that competed for my time. I worked without distractions just like any of the young men around me. Without meaning for it to happen, the title on my business card and I had become one. This upped the ante, however. If I lost my job now, I'd be losing much more than money. My very self and sense of worth were at stake. With so much on the line, I wasn't above burying a few principles in exchange for job security.

Over the years, I took many small vows of silence. Instead of speaking out, I learned to restrict my comments to a raised eyebrow, a cocked head, a thin smile. Sometimes these gestures had to pass for words when I was bursting to speak out against some perceived inequity, stupidity, or just plain old-fashioned monomaniacal egotism. One time, at a sales conference, I watched in silence as my boss's boss's boss swooped down on someone who worked for me. I knew his intentions were far from honorable. Indeed, within a few minutes, I saw the two of them leave the room together, and they were nowhere to be seen for an hour or so during the evening's festivities. Later that night, I found my young employee sitting by herself, a look of humiliation on her face as she realized that everyone knew what had just transpired. But I didn't stick up for her. I didn't complain, confront, or comment. My father, a very capable corporate veteran, had once warned me never to get into a pissing contest with someone taller than I was as I would be the one to get soaked. This was clearly one of those situations. Instead, I allowed my love of my job and my concerns about financial insecurity to justify my mute button. I turned the other way in silence.

As if fate were asking the question "How low can you go?" my own day of reckoning came not too long after that sales conference. I was in London on a business trip. I felt very glamorous, staying in Brown's Hotel, having tea with a British publisher. I sat quietly absorbed by a sense of sweet satisfaction.

That is, until one of my superiors walked in.

He wasn't supposed to be there. What, I wondered, *was* he doing here? Didn't he trust me? Didn't he think I could handle the publishing negotiation I had come to London to complete? I started to bristle. He sat down, ordered himself a vodka on the rocks, and began to talk. About nothing in particular. Three vodkas later, I still hadn't figured out what he was doing in London.

"Well," he said, more than a little tipsy. "We have to go to my room. It's late, and they won't serve us anymore."

"It's seven o'clock, and we're American business guests," I responded. "They'd serve us in the phone booth if we wanted." I didn't like where this conversation was going.

"No," he insisted, somewhat drunker than I'd guessed. (He must have had a head start before sitting down.) "We have to go upstairs."

It began to dawn on me that *I* was the point of his business trip.

"I will not go upstairs with you, and I'm going to give you the benefit of not knowing what you're saying due to being extremely drunk," I said as I scrambled for the high road. "Now, you go upstairs, and tomorrow we will pretend that this never happened."

"Then at least let me kiss that spot between your eyebrows."

For the next few weeks, I was a basket case. I loved my work and hated what was going on. I even despised the professional term for it: sexual harassment. I didn't want to be one of those women my male office peers referred to as "humorless" because we couldn't take a joke. (In fact, according to a 1997 report on sexual harassment conducted by the National Organization for Women, between 50 and 75 percent of all working women will experience sexual harassment while on the job. Nothing funny about that statistic.)

When I got back to the office, gifts started arriving—wallets, scarves—and I wondered whether I was being wooed or having my silence bought. I didn't know what to do. I knew one thing, though, for sure: I couldn't tell anyone, or I would lose my job and never, ever get another one.

I knew for a fact that if I so much as breathed a word, I would lose everything I had worked so hard for. I could put up with just about anything not to lose that. I began to rationalize. Gee, couldn't I start to look at this as sort of a compliment? It wasn't as if I couldn't do my job, and what really was the harm in it, and why couldn't I just have a sense of humor . . .

It's amazing what I had become willing to do to hold on to a job and a salary.

I'D BEEN COMPENSATED not just for my time or the quality of my work but for small and large acts of silence. The irony wasn't lost on me. I'd never made as much money before in my life, but I'd never traded more of myself for it. My search for independence had actually landed me in one of the most twisted relationships of my life. I found my continued employment dependent on keeping someone else's predatory behavior a secret. I kept his continued attempts to get me into bed hidden from my staff out of fear they would lose respect for me—a deception that made me complicit in his secret, loathsome behavior. I had to cover up for him. I learned to play by rules I abhorred. But the fear of losing my job, my place in the world, my identity—not to mention the economic security—silenced me. Compliance in exchange for money was an arrangement my father and men like him around the world had accepted for years. But it was not a value system I thought would ever apply to me.

And therein lies the rub: I, who would tell you straight to your face—and mean it—that money was not the most important thing in life, seemed to be increasingly willing to do just about anything to hold on to the job that provided it.

. . .

THIS WILLINGNESS INCLUDED working for far less than I was worth. Statistically speaking, women still earn only 78 percent of what men do, as noted earlier, and at our present glacial rate of progress it will take close to fifty years until we achieve parity.[1] There are a host of reasons why this is true: Women stop working to take care of kids; women move from full- to part-time work in order to take care of family. But the plain truth is—and it's not an easily quantifiable one—women don't fight for money the way men do.

We simply don't ask to be paid what we're worth. Lisa Barron, a professor of organizational behavior at the University of California, Irvine, conducted a study where she held mock job interviews and made salary offers to both men and women. She offered everyone $61,000 for the same job and then looked at the responses by gender. By the end of the negotiations, the men in the study had settled on an average salary of $68,556; the women, $67,000. Seventy percent of the men felt they were entitled to earn more than anyone else, while a similar percentage of women said they should earn what others earned. But most revealing, 85 percent of the men said they knew what they were worth. A similar number of women responded that they weren't sure.[2]

What makes this study even more remarkable is that all the participants were MBA students.

Women simply didn't feel comfortable thinking of themselves in monetary terms, Barron concluded. When asked to comment on these findings, Sheila Wellington, the president of Catalyst, an organization that focuses on the concerns of women and careers, observed, "Women have trouble tooting their own horns, shining a light on themselves. It shows up around salary."[3]

There's another distinctly female force at work that affects our salaries. It goes back to our hardwiring. Since it is in the nature of women to survive by keeping relationships and networks in working, mutually supportive order, behaviors that might involve pitting one person against another—even in the name of making more money—are not going to feel right or comfortable. This is one of the reasons that women rarely share salary information with one another. Doing so establishes instant hierarchies, which, by their very nature, put us on different planes from one another, thus separating us. We may not mind the fact that different levels exist, but we don't want another woman diminished by our success.

When we take the more affiliative, female perspective into organizational environments where the compensation and promotion systems were historically created for men, women wind up being penalized. We play by different rules with different criteria for what constitutes both success and acceptable behavior. Cutthroat behavior can be an asset even in a company that says it values teamwork. Most companies still operate by hierarchies, which are more natural constructs for men than for women.

Deborah Tannen, a linguistics professor at Georgetown University and author of the classic *You Just Don't Understand,* observes that gender can affect our compensation at work. "When hiring an employee, the employer knows that a man will take the job that pays him the most. But a woman will often take a lower-paying job because she likes other things about the job. This goes hand in hand with women having lower salaries. If a company can lure a woman without offering her more money than they have to, they certainly will."

Belinda, a senior executive at a big-city newspaper, was struck by the difference she found in men's and women's responses to her initial queries in her search for a new editor. "To a man (and I do mean that literally)," she told me, "every man I called was willing to meet with me to discuss the opening. They understood that even if they didn't want to leave their current positions, it couldn't hurt to make a good impression on a potential employer. I'm sure a few of them also thought they could parlay a job offer into a raise or promotion in their present positions."

Her experience with the women she approached couldn't have been more different. "More than half the women I called begged off even an introductory interview on the grounds that they just didn't feel they should waste my time. But I also got the distinct impression that they interpreted an interview as being disloyal to their current employers." Since one key way to get promoted and increase salary involves switching companies, these women are probably going to sacrifice position or money. This points out a fundamental difference in what women value. We are willing to sacrifice money for connection. But the trade hurts us financially.

To help explore some of these ideas further, I decided to send out a multiple-choice survey to a group of almost one hundred women whom I had identified through a financial self-help Web site. I wanted to know about how their emotions affected their money behavior in their love and work lives. When it came to the question "What do you most regret about your work experience?" the almost unanimous answer surprised me: Almost every woman had checked the box "I've not asked for enough money for work I've done."

Why not? What are we so afraid of? As I looked for an answer, I came across Elena, a single woman in her late fifties who had started her own freelance writing and editing company. Elena was about to fall into the economic abyss. She had so little money that friends had taken to bringing her food. As I talked to her, my heart broke. She'd been raised in poverty in Russia and had come to the United States to get an education and earn a living. She worked as a nurse's aide and went to college at night. After graduating, she took a job at a regional newspaper as a copy editor and stayed there for thirty years until she received an early retirement package when the paper fell on hard times and had to let go much of its staff.

Elena took the settlement and started her own business with it. But it hasn't supported her. She has work, but she won't charge enough to escape the slide into true poverty.

When I asked her what stops her from setting a fair price for her work, she told me she didn't know, but offered this story as an example. "A guy called the other day and asked me to fix a letter he'd written to his customers," she told me in a voice so soft it was often hard to hear her. "It was pretty good, although it needed editing. I could say to him, 'This is going to cost you $300 to revamp it,' but instead I called him up and told him, 'This is only going to take me an hour to do this, so I'm only going to charge you $100.'"

When I asked her why she didn't charge as much as she could get, she answered, "I can't possibly ask for that. It's too outrageous. I feel I should be asking as little as possible so I can make it right for him. That's the main thing—to make it right for the other person." Elena is afraid that if she asks for too much, she'll lose her client. But there's something more insidious going on. "There's a part inside me," she almost whispered, "that knows I'm selling myself out. But this little voice says, 'Make yourself as small as possible so they can't reject you. The less you want, the less you demand, the more they will keep you around.'"

Elena is going broke because she can't ask for what she thinks her work is worth. She has let her fear triumph over her needs. She resents it, she's mad at herself, but even those intense feelings aren't enough for her to challenge her belief that it's better to starve than lose a connection to another human being.

· · ·

CHELLIE CAMPBELL, a financial stress consultant, sees women like Elena—capable and terrified—in her workshops all the time. She points out that on top of our basic nature, the culture has not encouraged or prepared women to ask for money with the same ease as men. "Women aren't taught to be assertive and aggressive and go ask for money. They don't feel empowered to make money, and they aren't brought up to believe that money is a good thing. Women will often tell me when I ask them how their businesses are going, 'Well, I'm not in it for the money,' like that would be a bad thing. I think that's because women are supposed to be the nurturers and givers—it's better to give than to receive. We're brought up with that and we buy into it. 'You can't give from an empty cup,' I tell them. I urge them to stick up for themselves: 'Ask for money. Go get that raise. Set that price higher.' And they protest, 'But what about the poor and starving?' 'You can't help them by being one of them,' I tell them. 'The more you make, the more you can give and be of service.'"

Not wanting to see ourselves (or to be seen by others) as materialistic or selfish can also play a role in women's reluctance to ask to be paid as much as possible. After all, too many of us settle for recognition rather than remuneration. We're set up for this at the earliest ages. According to the financial expert Joline Godfrey, we simply aren't raised to think of ourselves as economic entities in the same way that young men are. When Godfrey talks to large groups of people, she often begins with this question: "How many of you had a business when you were kids?" If there are one hundred women in the room, usually five of them will raise their hands. "Then I will ask, 'How many of you were babysitters when you were kids?' About 85 percent of the women will raise their hands. I then will tell them, 'Well, think about it, you had a business. You were Sally Smith, Inc.,' and then the light dawns."

Godfrey feels we are fostering a strange schizophrenia in the culture when it comes to girls' and boys' financial abilities. Unwittingly, we don't encourage girls to think in economic terms. "If a girl is babysitting, and she's good at it, eventually somebody is going to say to her, 'You're so good with kids. Aren't you fabulous! You are just wonderful with children.' Meanwhile her brother is out there mowing lawns for cash, and nobody ever says to him, 'Aren't you good with lawns!' They say, 'Aren't you enterprising!' When we do this, we immediately give girls a sense of how good they are, as opposed to how resourceful and enterprising and entrepreneurial," she continues. "We frame their consciousnesses, and we frame their language. You see this on their first babysitting jobs when somebody asks, 'What are you going to charge me?' And even though girls are getting a little savvier, it's still more often than not, 'Um, I don't know. Whatever you want to pay me.' They feel so uncomfortable saying, 'I am worth this amount of money,' and it begins so early."

This discomfort, according to Godfrey, comes from the difference in girls' and boys' identities. "Women who don't have their financial selves together may feel incompetent or lack self-esteem, but they don't feel their womanhood is challenged. But a man who can't handle his finances feels his manhood is at stake." Because of these basic differences in how boys and girls assess their value in society, a boy who asks for money will be seen as a go-getter and a good earner. A girl may worry that she'll be regarded as a money-grubber.

I ask Godfrey why she thinks women go to such lengths to avoid the appearance of caring about how much they are compensated. "Don't you think that's a really good way to organize a society if you want some aspect of the society to take care of you for very little money?" she answers wryly. "Even though people deny it, it's terribly efficient."

These fundamental biological and sociological differences continue as young women enter the business world. We still aren't schooled, as young men are, in the mechanics of how to negotiate salaries or how to see money as a proxy for power and not a proxy for love or acceptance or another emotional need. Men often have mentors to pass along advice and experience. The financial consultant Pamela York Klainer recalls a couple she once interviewed. "She was a physicist. He was an executive. They worked together at Kodak, and both made good salaries. But one day the husband was pulled aside by a senior executive. 'Kodak gives a big bonus,' he was told. 'You want to start saving it in company stock.' Nobody said that to his wife. Here the husband was benefiting financially from the unwritten code of conduct among men to mentor other younger men. It's part of the deal. It's different for men to mentor women, and we, as executive women, do not do as good a job as the men. We don't pull younger women aside and tell them what's what."

Perhaps one reason we don't pass along hints about how to thrive at work is that women tend to feel ambivalent about the attitudes and behaviors that create success in many business environments. "Our culture worships work," Ann Crittenden reminds me. "It's a total workaholic culture, and you're fighting uphill against a whole value system when you say, 'Wait a minute. I have a family; I have a life.' Attitudes like 'It's all or nothing,' 'It's a hierarchy,' 'It's dog-eat-dog' prevail." And to adopt behaviors along those lines can turn us against ourselves in a clash of identity and values.

For all the changes in the work world in the last decades, it's undeniable that it still works best if you're a man or you have no children. The moment a working woman has a child, she's faced with the unlivable bargain that asks her to make trade-offs between the need to make money and the need to maintain her connection to her family. Balance eludes us not through any failing of our own but because structurally, work doesn't accommodate women's dual roles. "We can't integrate into the work structure as it is," Gloria Steinem once told me. "There is no such thing as integrating women equally into the economy as it exists. It's not possible. Not with all the other responsibilities women have. Not until the men are as equal inside the house as women are outside it. Not until we transform the system."

Further complicating and escalating what's at stake (beyond the anxiety-provoking fact that we need to make money) is that women derive both value and identity from the very thing that repels integration. We want and need meaningful work. But we also want and need balance. Too often, however, we have to sacrifice one for the other because of the way work and home lives are structured. And in doing so, we can feel like we're failing.

That's because we're judged (and we judge ourselves) by two mutually exclusive value systems. We know our success will be measured both by our work and by our ability to be "women." Society still judges us by how much money we make and by what kind of men we attract and what kinds of families we do or don't produce. "Put it this way: If you meet a woman who's doing wonderfully well professionally, doing great, creative things, and is completely happy with her work but she doesn't have the personal life she thinks she's supposed to have, she may think she's a failure," Steinem observed. "Men are the reverse. They can have great personal lives and think they're failures if they don't have the job success they think they're supposed to have."

Unfortunately, we internalize these conflicts and take them to the office with us every day. "I'll never forget it," Andrea, a thirty-year-old marketing director, tells me. "I knew I wanted to get pregnant, so I left my old job that I loved but that required tons of travel and took a job with a nonprofit organization. I figured, 'Good, I'll take less money if they promise me more flexibility and time off.'" But the benefits never materialized, and Andrea was furious. "Boy, did I mess up. I sacrificed money and then didn't get what I came for. And when I went to my boss and asked for either a raise or more time off than he'd offered, he told me that I wasn't being professional. So I got pregnant, took my time, and quit. But I didn't feel good about it. I guess I wasn't very professional about it after all."

Andrea's story may not have had a happy ending, but it contains a hopeful element: At least she went in to her boss and didn't censor herself when it came to asking for a raise. Indeed, things look like they're changing as younger generations have learned from their mothers' mixed successes. Today, women between the ages of twenty and twenty-four earn nearly 94 percent of men's salaries, whereas women who are forty-five to fifty-four years old earn 75 percent of what men do. [4]

"It's changing slowly," says the financial expert Jean Chatzky, referring to salary parity. "A lot of research has been done on the wage gap, and it all comes down to that very first salary discussion." As young women feel less constrained by traditional feminine behaviors and more valued for what they can contribute both at work and at home, this gap just might continue to close.

However, there is no way to measure whether we are making progress when it comes to other trade-offs—those self-censoring deals we make—silence for security, or charging too little for what we do in order to maintain the connection to the person or institution with the money. Goodness knows they don't work. They only serve to diminish us.

I EVENTUALLY LOST that job with the eyebrow-kissing executive in a corporate restructuring. He, too, soon left the company. I took a lower-level job that paid less but that promised a much saner environment. He went on to be a big success in a different field. I never said a word about what happened to anyone. I worked in publishing for many more years. Those two facts are not unconnected.

· 5 ·

YOU CAN NEVER BE
TOO RICH OR TOO THIN

I DATED ONLY TWO MEN WHO MADE MORE MONEY THAN
I did, and I married the second one. I would have happily
married the first since he was my inaugural big love, but (a)
he didn't ask me and (b) much to my surprise, it turned out
he was already married to someone else (which might
explain why he didn't ask). There was a third man who *had*
more money than I did (due to a sizable inheritance), but he
didn't *make* more. (Thus, while still appealing, the fact that
he hadn't made it himself placed him in a slightly different
category.) Nevertheless, I would have married him too, but
the question likewise never passed his lips. As much as I
would like to believe that money didn't factor in when it
came to dating and mating, I can't honestly say that it's true.

My dating years were a little more extended than I'd
hoped. I was thirty-five by the time someone finally proposed to me. (I always quietly feared that my economic

independence was the turnoff.) Sometimes I dated for love (or the lust that passes for it temporarily). There were actor-waiters, writer-waiters, and composer-waiters who made no reliable money and whose prospects for ever doing so were extremely slim. Occasionally, I dated men with some economic promise: a magazine editor, a TV reporter, and a guy who traded currencies. I never quite made the rounds of bankers, stockbrokers, or lawyers. Rather than risk the rejection I was sure would come if I stuck a toe in those distilled waters, I ceded them to the women they favored anyway, the ones who were born to wear little black sleeveless cocktail dresses without having to put something over their upper arms to hide the extra pouch of skin that no amount of aerobics classes seemed to vanquish.

So it was to my great surprise when the attractive man on the M5 bus with the lopsided smile leaned over and whispered the answer to 35 Down in the daily crossword puzzle. I'd smelled him first. It had been raining, and his nicely tailored gray herringbone coat smelled of wet wool, rich and musky. *"Edify,"* he said. His eyes looked right into mine from no more than eighteen inches away. They were green with flecks of orange.

"Thanks," I said, looking down in order to simultaneously check his left hand (no wedding ring) and his shoes (nice, expensive business-type wing tips). Here was a handsome man with brains and, judging by his footwear, a good job.

I don't know what appealed to me most, but the fact that

he didn't look like he depended on gratuities for a living definitely factored into my swift interest in this most promising candidate for the man who would sweep me up, marry me, and make sure that whatever work I did in the future would be for love, not money.

I fell hard for this interesting man—a lawyer, but on his way into the real estate business. We lunched; we talked; my fingers never touched a check in any restaurant. He paid for cabs; he paid for drinks. I never felt so taken care of in all my adult life. Within days, I was picking out my wedding dress, thinking about what kind of friends we'd have, what kind of kids, what kind of home. Here was a man who was not only engaging but solvent. Solvent enough to be a great candidate for marriage.

Then, one day about five weeks into our relationship, we went for a bike ride. He showed up in front of my apartment building wearing a rust-orange turtleneck, a pair of beaten-up brown corduroys, and riding an old-fashioned three-speed bike with a child's seat on the back. A *what*? I reran the tapes. Had I missed the kid part, or had he neglected to tell me he had any? There were two, as it turned out. And a wife. Only one of those, but that was one too many for me. The man I married shouldn't already be married. That much I knew.

"Honestly, I can explain," he said. "We're separated."

I was so in love both with him and with my fantasy that, for a time, I let myself believe him. Even years later, long after he went back to his wife (which I wanted him to do— not because I wasn't crazy about him but because I didn't want to break up a marriage), I was unable to completely untangle the emotional strings that kept us connected. For almost twenty years, he occupied a corner of my heart, and I couldn't entirely give up the idea of him.

What does this have to do with money? Nothing directly, but rarely do we admit to ourselves—no less anyone else—money's immediate power to seduce. Of course there were other things that attracted me to him, but financial abundance cannot be discounted. This man didn't buy me jewels or take me on expensive trips, but his confidence, his protective way of putting his hand on the small of my back and directing me through a door, the quiet power that rolled off him signaled that he was the kind of guy who knew how to make sure the woman he loved felt secure.

As the years passed, when I was in the middle of a dating dry spell or at the end of yet another disappointing relationship experience, I would let my mind drift back to this powerful man and imagine how easy my life would have been as his wife. His ultimate prominence (it wasn't long before I started seeing his name regularly in the newspapers and in magazines) meant I wouldn't have had to work, put up with crazy bosses, or worry about paying my rent with a check that I knew would bounce. In my dreams, this man had become the piece that filled both the hole in my heart and the one in my pocket. Long after our affair ended, the tantalizing fantasy of the comfortable life lingered in my dreams. Our conversations, even our lovemaking, didn't. I suppose that says it all.

· · ·

ALMOST FROM THE time we're conscious, girls get messages about the kind of men we're supposed to date and then marry. These messages become all tangled up in the picture of the life we're supposed to lead. We're told both directly and indirectly what constitutes a good candidate for husband and provider, and what makes a guy a great date but a bad bet for a lifetime partner. These tiny time capsules of cultural and economic information rest quietly in us and explode later in our dating lives as we come in contact with potentially viable (or impossible) men.

Not surprisingly, money factors heavily into these directives. We should marry someone like our fathers (assuming that they were good providers), or we should marry men who were nothing like them (in the case that they were no good, they didn't earn enough, or they squandered what they did bring in). We are supposed to marry for love (didn't we hear the romantic stories of how our parents met?), yet it was wisest to marry someone who could "take care of us," because, after all, marriage wasn't about love but about security and occasionally social position. (My grandmother married my grandfather for both, yet their decades of mutual disdain began as early as their wedding night, when she woke up to find him naked on the floor calling football plays in his sleep. Nonetheless, they stayed married for almost sixty years.)

What I didn't hear at home, I picked up from cultural messages that were like wallpaper in every room of my young life. Many of the movies I watched as a little girl had a rescuer or a Prince Charming. If he wasn't obviously a prince, he turned out to be one in disguise. (The movies that didn't feature rescuers inevitably starred spunky tomboy girls who could take care of themselves, thus telegraphing the split many of us would feel later as adult women.)

To catch one of these princes, however, a woman had to accomplish three mythic tasks, just like in the fairy tales: She had to be thin, she had to be beautiful, and she couldn't be too threatening (that is, there had to be a streak of neediness and vulnerability in there somewhere). Even though I outwardly rejected this formula, I couldn't completely side-step the message that the purpose of dating was not only to find my true love but to make myself attractive enough to get some permanent economic security.

"That's because for a woman, from a survival-of-the-species point of view, the need for financial security is numbers one, two, and three," explains the psychiatrist Louann Brizendine. "There are all sorts of ways that women go about getting this security from different mates—like being attractive, exchanging sexual favors—and it's all driven by this core imperative. But when fulfilling a basic, primitive need doesn't match up with the higher self a woman has in mind, the result is a conflict. Any time there's a cultural value that doesn't fit with our biology, we're going to engage this conflict. The feelings that result are stronger than guilt. We feel shame."

Brizendine observes that the conflict causes us to avoid looking directly at the financial side of dating because it brings up these shameful feelings we don't like. "Women don't talk about money when it comes to men and financial safety—not only because it's part of our unconscious, our ancestry, and our genes, but because we feel it takes away from the romantic ideal. It doesn't match up with how we want things to be. Women in our culture have been told that the ideal is the romantic-love marriage. If other things intrude—like crass money issues—we feel they sully everything, and then we feel ashamed about that." We may not like to admit that money plays a role in dating but that doesn't diminish the power of the "core" drive for security. Instead, our discomfort pushes this influence out of sight, where it sits invisibly influencing our dating choices.

On the other hand, our culture elevates another part of this biological imperative: Women are fed the repeated message that our youth and looks are the tickets to love and economic stability. By the time a girl is seventeen, she'll have been bombarded by a quarter of a million advertisements directed at improving her appearance.[1] These ads emphasize good hair, nice skin, white teeth, and a slender yet curvy body—ideals best achieved with youth. The explosion of teen magazines (like *Cosmo Girl* and *Young Vogue*) are training wheels for the later style vehicles that make the direct connection between a woman's physical assets and her romantic and sexual life.

No one in my family ever connected the beauty/youth/security dots directly. It was more subtle than that. But there was nothing understated about what I heard and saw in the media that featured magazine headlines that tease with tips like "The Sexual Position That He Secretly Wants You to Try!" While these "tips" weren't expressed as direct economic equations that traded sex for security, if I paid careful attention, I would see that the next boldfaced headline on the magazine's cover probably had something to do with how to best catch a man. (The headline refers to an actual *Cosmo* article that reveals that men secretly like sex best when women are on top. But the article points out that women don't prefer that position because it makes it easier for the man to actually *see* the woman's body, which, her insecurity tells her, might make her less appealing. Less appealing means less likely to marry. And even if the woman has no interest in marrying the man, she is still probably interested in knowing she could marry him if she wanted to. Sex and money. Sex for power. Dating for dollars. The oldest of unspoken equations.)

"I REALIZED THE other day that now, when I meet a guy, if he's going to law school or has some money or something like that, all of a sudden, I'm much more interested," muses Laura, a twenty-two-year-old who has just graduated from college. We're sitting on a fence railing in the middle of an organic farm. This slight young woman with the waist-long braids, ripped-up jeans, and manure-encrusted boots does not look like someone who would care about her boyfriend's annual income. She's planning on going to graduate school in public policy but has taken the year off to live in a commune and work on the land. "I have every intention of working. I don't think of myself as money loving or anything like that, but if a guy can pay for stuff, it's kind of hot. Both my parents worked, so it's not like I expect a man to provide for me; that wasn't how it was in my house at all. But there's just something about a guy who takes making money seriously. It's like he's a grown-up and can handle himself. I like that. It makes me feel safe."

Admitting that money is an aphrodisiac may rank among the most politically incorrect confessions a woman can make.

But that doesn't make it any less real.

Young women in their late teens and early twenties seem to be having fewer problems than some of their mothers admitting that money matters when it comes to dating and mating. Joline Godfrey worries about the misconceptions many of the young women she's talked with have about what lies ahead on this path. "Ten years ago, when I first started consulting, I remember saying to friends, 'I'm only going to be doing this for a short while because younger women won't need to be told about the repercussions of economic dependency.' Now, what really frightens me is that I can walk into any private school and many of the middle- and upper-middle-class public schools in America, and a minimum of a third of the girls—sometimes many more—will say, 'Take care of myself? Ugh. I'm just going to marry rich.'" It's like a time warp back to a mentality that is simply shocking in light of the real information that 90 percent of women have to take care of themselves at some point in their lives.

According to Godfrey, it's not only the affluent young women who feel this way. "It's everywhere you look. Especially in the media. The new celebrants are the 'celebu-tantes'; whether it's Paris Hilton or these kids who are being covered on the E! Entertainment Network as having these amazing well-dressed-mucho-bling-party-every-night lives that are seemingly supported by magic." Godfrey tells me that she would love to think this is an upper-middle-class phenomenon because then she wouldn't worry so much about it. But the problem is that because of the media, this idolatry cuts across every economic class. "It doesn't matter how much your mother makes, you are still watching the same role models on MTV. That's the most insidious part. Regardless of where your family stands on the financial spectrum, you're getting blasted by the same cultural messages as everybody else. Kids grow up thinking, 'That's how people live—I deserve to live like that.'"

MY VANITY MIGHT protest that money didn't affect my dating choices, but then how do I explain my relationship with "the Scion"? I'd always liked Charlie; I'd known him for years. He was a gentle soul, a funny guy, a political activist with just enough of a dark side to save him from being the kind of person I would feel guilty being around because he was so good. Charlie also had two country houses, a penthouse apartment in the city, and a sailboat. These things cannot be discounted when it came to attraction. When I looked at him, I saw all his lovely qualities. He just didn't light my world on fire, and to be honest, I didn't seem to be the answer to his fantasies either. I was more than happy to trade our strangely dispassionate life for one of security and comfort, though. Especially since he was such a great guy. We agreed on politics, on lifestyles, and seemed more like great siblings than ardent lovers. Charlie took me to England and Greece and Ireland, something that I, with my $21,000 salary, could not have afforded. I was so anxious that he ask me to marry him, I missed one of my closest friend's weddings because we were in Ireland and I was trying to procure an invitation to my own.

I did what many women do in this circumstance: I blamed my failure on my figure. Charlie had once remarked that maybe our sex life would be a little hotter if I lost ten pounds. I'd thoroughly bought into the economic calculus that says the less you weigh, the better your chances will be of "marrying well," as my grandmother would have said. Clearly, for Charlie, I tipped the scale ten pounds past marriage potential. The message was, lose weight or be responsible for my own finances for the rest of my life.

I became addicted to my exercise class. I lived on lettuce and nonfat cottage cheese. I learned how to throw up. I smoked cigarettes. I lost the ten pounds. Then another ten. Still no "Will you marry me?" was forthcoming. I got so mad at being inadequate to the challenge of becoming a bride that I rebelled against Charlie. I double-timed him, falling hard for a starving artist. I turned into such an emotional and physical train wreck that Charlie ultimately gave me the heave-ho—as he should have. I didn't get a husband, but I did get an ulcer, which landed me in the hospital for two weeks with liquid Valium dripping through an IV into my arm.

An equation unequivocably exists between a woman's youth and beauty and her economic condition. "The economic power of a twenty-two-year-old woman probably outweighs that of a like-aged man because she has youth and beauty to trade for the man's currency," Gloria Steinem once told me. (She went on to say, however, that it was a lousy bargain because any $50 that woman would earn on her own would be better than $500 from a man that would make her dependent.)

The media broadcasts standards of beauty around the world. Not only does a young woman have to be thin; she has to have a shape not found in nature. American television shows aired abroad feature twig-thin women with ample breasts. This has inspired an international trend of body makeovers. According to the *London Daily Telegraph,* the number of British women who underwent cosmetic operations rose by more than 50 percent between 2003 and 2004.[2] And in America, cosmetic surgery on young women has risen steeply and steadily for the past decade. Between 2002 and 2003 alone, the number of girls eighteen years old and younger who got breast implants nearly tripled, according to the American Society for Plastic Surgery.[3]

While these young women may be seeking approval, pleasure, or satisfaction in their looks, it's another question entirely about what motivates them to conform to cultural ideals of femininity. Since beautiful women attract men—and potential husbands—it isn't too far a stretch to suggest that these young women may be unconsciously seeking a return on their surgical investments. In dating, as in work, as women try to resolve their conflicts between their drives for security and for independence, they still know that resorting back to old "feminine" stereotypes pays off.

˝I HAD NEVER gone out with someone for money, and I had never dated an older man," Anita, a statuesque brunette in her midthirties, tells me with a disbelieving shake of her head. "But Martin was extremely charming, very taken with me, and he spoiled me rotten. I'd never gone for rich men, so it was such a novelty to me. I remember he sent me a really gorgeous gold bracelet after I first met him in a Barnes & Noble. My sister told me to send it back immediately, and I said, 'Oh, can't I keep it? I've never had anything like this in my whole life.' Then she begged me to give it back. But I said, 'No. I don't want to. I want to keep it.' I figured I could find a way to like him.

"Here was this guy—someone who sent his driver to drop off gifts at my office or at home—gold jewelry, exotic flowers, invitations to formal brunches, and plane tickets. It was like a fairy tale. I was almost thirty, and he was in his sixties. He walked with a cane; he looked like a cadaver."

Anita dated her magnate for a year. But then her boss sat her down and had a heart-to-heart talk. "She told me that I was on an upward curve with my career, and were I to get more involved and marry this man, my career would just be gone. This guy had so much money that if I married him, I would become a shadow. I would be insignificant. That got my full attention. I realized I'd rather make my own money than roll around in his. So I tried to pull back. But this guy freaked out. He followed me around for a year after I broke up with him. It drove me into therapy because I was having violent dreams about men. I melted down a big gold bracelet he gave me and got about $400 for it. I began to see that no amount of money would make up for a guy that possessive. He was almost stalking me. It took me a while to trust enough to date again, and when I finally felt safe enough, I went out and found someone where I could be the principal wage earner. I don't want to be controlled by a guy's money ever again."

Anita eventually ended up marrying a guy "for love, not money," she says. "I learned my lesson." Her husband, a news photographer, makes a fraction of the money her old boyfriend made. "I adore Josh," she reports, "but I have to be honest. I would like it if he were exactly the way he is but really rich."

Sometimes we don't even know that we're attracted to someone because he's telegraphing all the attributes of a promising financial mate. "My mother always used to say, 'Be careful. You're going to wind up in the poorhouse!' It was like a reverse affirmation," thirty-two-year-old Ellen tells me over an iced tea. We're sitting in a small bistro having lunch not far from her new apartment in a nice part of St. Louis. The restaurant is full of women—some in pairs, some with kids, some with their mothers. There are few men around. It's the middle of the day in the middle of the week. "My father came from nothing but he's very pragmatic, and I'm not the most practical soul. He worries about me."

Ellen had met Jason, a lawyer, at an event for singles. He had on a nice pair of slacks, a pressed shirt, and a confident way of asking if she wanted something to drink. They began dating and within a year became engaged. When I ask Ellen how important money was in her attraction to Jason, she says that she didn't know how much money he had until after he'd asked her to marry him. It turned out he had an inheritance, but she hadn't explicitly known that. "I think it was an attraction to money at more of a subconscious level," she tells me.

Looking back, she now realizes that even though she wasn't aware of it at the time, Jason sent messages about his wealth in quiet, indirect ways. Ellen says she knew his family was financially stable and that he hadn't had to worry about money. His parents had paid for law school. "I didn't look at him and see a rich guy; instead, I internalized the aura more as secure. I didn't consciously think that stability equaled money at the time. Now I see it was clearly all related, but I wasn't seeing it all at that point. I was missing the big thing— that money didn't make him mature. When it came down to it, though, he just couldn't commit to me. It was like pulling teeth to get him to ask me to marry him. I decided I couldn't stay in the relationship because he was clearly not stable if he could waffle that much on something like getting married."

Ellen's mother worries about her and wonders if the relative comfort in which Ellen was raised has left her unprepared for financial responsibility. Her mother knows what it's like to lose everything and fears Ellen will follow in her path. Ellen's mother grew up in a wealthy family, but her father made some poor business decisions shortly before his death and lost all the family money in a matter of months. And it's not lost on Ellen that with her recent heartbreak, she's had an echo of her mother's experience. Getting married would have bailed Ellen out of some debts she'd incurred. She's always lived slightly outside her means, more because she's chosen work that doesn't pay well than because she spends too much. She worked in the Peace Corps and then became a teacher. "I do worry about money. But I also have limits about what I'm willing to do for it. I watched your generation," she says, referring to those of us approaching our fifties. "I know you can't have it all, so I want to have a life that means something to me. But now I see my own contradictions. Unconsciously, I thought I was going to be like my mother and marry someone who eventually was going to take care of me even though I had a career."

Ellen admits that part of her must have wanted that option of being taken care of. But at what cost? "My ex-future mother-in-law was a real nightmare. She never thought I was good enough for her son. But somehow I

thought it would all work out. At first, I was willing to kow-
tow and contort. I lost nineteen pounds and ended up with
irritable bowel syndrome. But I was socialized to think this
was okay. On a certain level, I must have been saying to
myself, 'I'm going to put up with this because the payoff is
going to be good.' It's this weird thing where we invest in
men, but I hadn't registered any of this. I wasn't Miss
Wallflower. I'd worked overseas and all across the country,
but on some subconscious plane I just assumed that eventually the financial picture would just work itself out in a
relationship."

Ellen falls silent, and as I look around the restaurant, I
notice that none of the women look like they're getting up
from their meals and rushing off to an office somewhere.
The irony isn't lost on Ellen. She's clearly registering that
the women sitting around us are living the life she almost
embraced. After a minute or so, she continues talking. "I
knew intellectually that men weren't necessarily the payout,
and I knew that a relationship wasn't going to rescue me. I
knew all of this before I got engaged. But I hadn't realized
how much baggage came along with the money issue,
whether it was in a relationship or in my own life. There's a
weird entitlement thing I've internalized, and I resent it.
'Do I really have to know about financial matters?' I ask
myself. 'Won't somebody else eventually take care of this for
me? Why do I need to know this?' I have to admit there is
some resentment that I have to take on my financial life."

Celia, a forty-nine-year-old media planner, echoes Ellen's
ambivalent feelings. Now that she's past her childbearing

years, her dating focus has shifted from finding a husband who might provide for her to finding a companion so she won't be alone. "I went on a few of those Web sites," she says. "But the guys who are interested in women my age are either really old or total losers. I went on a couple of dates where I had to pay half. Please spare me!" Celia thinks she's never gotten married because men find her to be "too much." She made too much money, talked too much, "was too out-there." "They like me in bed," she says with a shake of her highlighted auburn hair. "But I'm not the kind of girl they were going to marry. I didn't 'need' them enough. Maybe I should have played things down, but then, that's not who I am."

Celia is convinced that she's paid a price for having been herself. She has no doubt that had she been a skinny, feminine, dependent girl like one of her sisters-in-law, she'd be married with a family today. "Maybe I go after the wrong guys," she says. "Maybe I wanted too much. I wanted funny and smart and successful. Who knows?"

I recognized her despair. Somewhere around my thirtieth birthday, I too had begun to wonder if something was wrong with my man-picker skills. I couldn't seem to find one who was interested in me and also had both the means and the manner that fit my dreams. So it was with great relief that within a few years, through mutual friends, I met the man who would become my first husband. At last, I thought, a match. Someone handsome enough, smart enough, strong enough, manly enough, and, yes, liquid enough, to qualify as my would-be rescuer. Yes, I was supposed to marry for love, but as my grandmother had pointed out long ago, loving a rich man is just as easy as loving a poor one.

During all that time that I trolled in earnest for a husband, I'm not sure I had the maturity to recognize that two kinds of rich exist: bank account abundance and wealth of the spirit. While they don't have to be mutually exclusive, the first time around I'd wildly undervalued the kind of wealth that can't pay for a honeymoon in Paris.

· 6 ·

FOR RICHER OR POORER

MOST OF MY FRIENDS WERE MARRIED LONG BEFORE I ever got near an altar (not counting the six supportive trips I made down the aisle in traditionally hideous bridesmaid dresses). From the cheap seats, I'd had the chance to watch what happened when money concerns started to wiggle their way into the marriages. When they stood there vowing to love each other "for richer or poorer," I was never sure whether the fact that they were essentially entering into a financial arrangement was foremost in their minds.

Ruth and Michael were the first to take the plunge, which they did to the strains of Percy Sledge blasting "When a Man Loves a Woman" from a portable tape player. Technically, there was no aisle or altar. Instead, the wedding took place in the all-night Greek diner where they'd had their first date two years earlier, as college seniors. Ruth wore some strange artistic construction she'd designed. (A sculptress, she worked for an art director in an ad agency to pay her bills.) Michael, a painter content with his penury, sported white tie and tails borrowed from the college's drama department, where he worked from time to time painting sets. We drank champagne and ate pancakes and sausages. The whole affair had a dress-up, make-believe aspect to it. They were both twenty-four, in love, and flat broke.

They married each other's promise—neither one of which turned out as expected. For the first two or three years, they enjoyed the bohemian, starving-artist life. But slowly, Ruth became more committed to her work at the agency, which she didn't mind too much since she'd ended up on an account that pushed her creatively. Michael continued painting large, confrontational pictures. Sometimes Ruth and I would meet up after work, and a couple of years into the marriage I began to notice strains of frustration slipping into her voice as she talked about coming home to coffee cups that hadn't moved from the sink to the dish drainer even though Michael had been home all day with nothing to do but drag a brush across a canvas.

They had their first big fight three years into their marriage, when Ruth discovered she was pregnant. "I didn't want to raise a baby in a loft with all those paint smells," she recalls. Or have to walk up four flights toting the kid. "I told him he had to get a job, that I couldn't support the family and work full-time, and that I wanted to move." But Michael had no interest in getting a job. He'd never had a job. Had never planned to. "That was a moment of awakening for me," Ruth remembers. "I felt like a fool. My respect for him sunk to an all-time low. It was clear that I was the one who was going to have to be the grown-up, the 'responsible' one. He wasn't going to do it. We'd talked about all this before, but when the rubber met the road, he was just going to let me do it."

Ruth, facing either the loss of the partner she'd hoped for or the loss of her actual husband, went with the former. She packed away her sculptures, accepted a promotion at work, and settled in to her new role as the one who made the money. "I resented it, and I probably held it over his head," she says. "I think that's why he had the affair with the woman he ended up sharing a studio with. But I was pissed."

Their relationship hit its lowest point soon after their daughter was born. "To tell the truth, I had very little use for him at that time," she says, "and we really didn't see eye to eye about what kind of life we wanted to lead. I wanted to live in a decent home where I didn't have to step over bums to get to my door. He said that I was being bourgeois. But I made the money. I told him that he'd given up his vote when he decided he wouldn't support the family." Ruth tells me she has no idea what kept them married through that experience. "Maybe I was too tired to get a divorce," she suggests sarcastically.

I remember watching this drama unfold, while my friends and I took turns pointlessly urging Michael to get a job, *do* something. Ruth was growing unpleasantly bitter; he was acting like an immature, spoiled prince. It wasn't pretty.

Then a blackout curtain fell between Ruth and Michael and their friends, and they retreated behind it to work out their marriage. In private.

Michael emerged with an application to architecture school. Ruth went to work, making enough money to pay for a move to a nondescript two-bedroom apartment in a more family-friendly part of town. I have no idea what bargain they made or what they renegotiated in their relationship. But it must have worked because twenty-five years later, they're still married. Ruth continues to make most of the money and, to the outside eye, appears to control the material side of their life, but they seem to live very peacefully. "I didn't need him to make the money" is all she'll say on the subject. "I just needed him to try. To participate. To act in a way that I could respect. Sitting on his ass at home wasn't going to cut it." I've never asked Michael about his side of the agreement. I guess part of me just doesn't want to know. He's had a modestly successful career in a firm that remodels high-end retail stores. He's never sold a painting.

EVERY MARRIAGE HAS power struggles in which money becomes the rope in the tug-of-war between conflicting wills, desires, and fears. After all, a marriage is a contract, and a contract expects and demands something from each participant. We want to know that the other person, whose destiny is now tied to ours, has his or her head screwed on straight about the responsible use of what becomes mutual cash. But this is where that conflict erupts again between our materialism and our desire to place a higher value on other things in life. Marriage may be a financial union as much as one of the heart, but most of us steadfastly refuse to look at it that way—until we have to.

None of my friends had prenuptial agreements (but then again, none of them had any money). They all married for love, but each had hidden expectations about who was going to support whom and how. Ruth married Michael for his passion and creativity but ended up resenting him for being passionate and creative and wholly uninterested in the more traditional role of provider-husband. The nonmaterial qualities she wanted in a lover fell short of the material responsibilities dictated by fatherhood. When their lives changed, different expectations arose.

Even though Ruth was the breadwinner (a role women now play in one out of every three marriages with working spouses),[1] she and Michael ended doing something that almost every married couple does: They developed compensatory spending styles. In a marriage, no matter where we start out, our anxieties about finance, our questions about whether we can truly trust our spouse with money, pull us with the force of emotional gravity into complementary roles. Each spouse takes on the characteristics of the Hoarder or Spender, the Worrier or Dreamer, the Responsible One or Magical Thinker. Even two people who start out in the same place in most cases will eventually take on opposing roles. Money, because it carries power in a marriage, forces these counterbalances.

Sometimes it takes a long time for these conflicts to come into focus. It's downright unromantic to talk about cash and issues like who's going to provide for whom and how; after all, almost nine out of ten of us dream of marrying our soul mates—not our providers, according to a Rutgers University study.[2] But once we get into the actual business of paying for our joint lives, we start to see the force that money exerts and the compensating inevitably begins.

We come into our marriages with a wealth of experiences and expectations—often unconscious and therefore unarticulated—about what constitutes appropriate fiscal behavior in a spouse. We can't help but judge our mates by them. The degree to which our husbands conform to our often unspoken expectations contributes to—or detracts from—the level of trust we have in their ability to make and manage money. When they act as we feel they should, we trust them. When they don't, an endless series of anxious nights can ensue.

By the time Anne fell in love with David, he'd defaulted on two credit cards. Between the charges and the interest, he owed Visa almost $20,000. She was understanding, though. After all, he hadn't spent the money on anything frivolous. After his divorce, he'd had to start all over again, buying furniture, silverware, toasters, and mattresses. She didn't mind dating his debt, but when he asked her to marry him, she realized his outstanding balances—and his "who-gives-a-fig" attitude—upset her. It didn't make her feel safe and threatened to lessen her respect for him. She told him that until he dealt with his debt, marriage wasn't an option. "I never even have a balance," she says with a shudder. "I can't stand owing money."

Every few days, Anne would ask David if he'd settled with the creditors. David, being a bit of a procrastinator, kept promising he would. But each time he couldn't give Anne the answer she wanted, she'd tuck the information away. His reluctance to be responsible (in her opinion) never left her peripheral vision. Finally, David, his back against a wall, called the creditors and negotiated a payment. "Ten cents on the dollar!" he crowed. Anne felt deflated. He didn't get it. It wasn't about the debt so much as it was about taking responsibility. The man she married shouldn't need her to tell him what was right and wrong—especially where money was concerned. She didn't want to financially babysit him. It was a turnoff.

"It's a huge company," David exclaimed. "It's not as if I make a difference to them." Anne felt vaguely nauseous. This wasn't how she grew up. In her family, men didn't try to discount their financial responsibilities. Paying what you owed was a sign of fiscal solvency and emotional maturity. When David first ducked his creditors and then made a deal with them, Anne felt like he was making others pay for his irresponsible behavior.

When they finally married (after David was free and clear of his debt), Anne adamantly refused to put their money together. She wanted nothing to do with his approach to finance. This arrangement worked for fifteen years.

But one day, Anne accidentally opened a letter addressed to David. It was from a collection agency and listed no fewer than five credit cards—all maxed out. She confronted her husband, who admitted that over the years, he'd simply let the debt creep up again. At first she pushed him: Was there another woman? Did he have a gambling problem? Online sex charges? No, it turned out to be nothing nearly so interesting, just run-of-the-mill overspending.

They debated declaring bankruptcy, but Anne couldn't stomach the thought. So she came up with a novel solution: Since they had no children, she decided to divorce David so she wouldn't be responsible for any future debt. "We're still together, but legally, I want nothing to do with his problems. I'm on the hook for the old charges, but going forward he's on his own."

In 1940, two-thirds of all married couples in the United States adhered to the conventional arrangement in which the husband worked and the wife stayed at home. By 2002, that figure had plummeted to 16 percent.[3] Yet attitudes about who should control the money have lagged behind. When *Redbook* and *Smart Money* magazines polled men and women between the ages of eighteen and fifty, the majority of both sexes felt the husbands had better money judgment than their spouses.[4]

No one wants to admit that they don't have faith in their spouse's ability to handle money, but ultimately, if it's there, that distrust always emerges. It may do so indirectly, but it sits there like a lemon slowly rotting on the kitchen counter. Sometimes our mates do something to earn our wariness, and sometimes we enter our marriages with vigilance as a result of bad experiences. This loss of trust sets off big issues between couples. What starts as a money problem can grow into bigger marital questions about whether a spouse feels loved enough or feels powerless in the marriage. Both men and women commingle money and power, but they do so differently. For women, money, romantic love, and being taken of are all tied together. A woman is more likely to interpret differences in opinion about how to deal with an investment or debt as a lack of consideration or concern on her husband's part. She might react to an inexpensive birthday present as if it were a demonstration of insufficient love or a lavish one as proof of affection. She might find an independent purchase on the man's part a sign of emotional distance.

The linguistics expert Deborah Tannen offers an example of how differently men and women can interpret something as common as buying a new desktop computer. "One source of distress and conflict in many couples I found was that men would go out and make a big purchase without checking with their wives, whereas women would never do that. It wasn't that women necessarily objected to the specific purchase that their husbands made as much as they objected to their making a unilateral decision. A woman will check in with her husband because for her, that communication signals a partnership, a connection, and a sense that 'we're in this together.' But for a man, checking with a woman about a purchase means he's asking for permission, which is what you do with a parent, not a spouse. Where she feels connected, he feels infantilized."

While most of these power struggles appear to be about spending and saving, there's often another, deeper dimension. Because of the changes that have occurred over the last fifty years, there's an enormous collective emotional confusion about who is supposed to provide what in a marriage. "While men today are supposed to accept the fact that women make money and have power, it's not like they've been released from that role either," Stephen Goldbart points out. "What men expect from themselves and what women expect from men has hardly changed." This, Goldbart says, has left couples with inconsistent sets of assumptions, with each spouse having unconscious expectations of how the other spouse is supposed to behave. The result can be conflict and confusion.

When we feel at odds with our spouses about money—especially if children are involved—seemingly insignificant differences in spending habits can feel like enormous emotional threats. Paula, a forty-two-year-old Internet marketing executive who lives in Silicon Valley, says she felt her children's very future was at stake when she discovered just how much a home renovation had exceeded its budget. When Paula was pregnant with their second child, she and her husband, Peter, realized that they would have to expand their small 1930s bungalow. As it was, they were bursting at the seams. Peter, a contractor, decided to take the opportunity to turn their house into a showcase for his work and drew up extensive plans that he showed to Paula in her first trimester. "I was sick as a dog," says Paula. "I wasn't focusing on things like hand-tooled banisters and computerized controls for all the rooms."

The first warning sign came when Paula, who made more money than Peter, realized they couldn't live in the house during construction—an expense for which Peter hadn't budgeted. "If he hadn't considered something as fundamental as that—I was pregnant after all—I began to question his judgment about other decisions. I wanted to go through everything, item by item, for my peace of mind. He had ridiculous things in there—a marble bathroom for the kids. They are kids! I'd rather put the money in their education, not on their walls."

What Paula now sees is that Peter interpreted her questions about certain design decisions and her pleas for cost-cutting as attacks on his abilities as a builder, and thus on him as a man and husband. In her mind, she was just trying to keep things simple and save as much as she could. Both had the happiness of the family in mind. Peter wanted to provide a beautiful home, and Paula wanted to keep their savings intact.

Their marriage didn't survive the renovation.

· · ·

COUPLES ARE CHANGING how they handle their finances by revisiting roles and expectations. Separate bank accounts—virtually unheard of two generations ago—are now common. Keeping finances separate is sometimes an effective way to accommodate different spending styles and priorities in a marriage. As long as that arrangement can be maintained, couples can usually avoid conflicts. Amy and Andy are a perfect example. Amy came from an affluent family, Andy from a working-class background. Amy's mother spent lavishly and impulsively, a behavior that Andy disapproved of. He also worried that Amy might inherit her mother's wasteful ways. Even though Amy had never shown the least desire to buy things she didn't need simply because they were on sale, he still eyed her suspiciously each time she came home with a shopping bag in hand. Amy resented his inquiries about every purchase she made.

"Do I ask you about how much your fancy gym costs each month?" Amy asked with no small irritation. "I don't know who you're responding to; it isn't me. You're acting out of fear I will become my mother. When I start eating and spending compulsively, then worry. Until then, this is me you're dealing with, not my mother!"

Amy, a devoted Democrat, had her own irritations with some particular aspects of Andy's spending. He was a passionate Republican who abhorred every penny of tax he had to pay; he felt the government was taking food out of his children's mouths. One day, Amy found an entry in the check registry for a $100 contribution to the National Republican

Party. "That was it for me," she recalls. "I was not paying for that. I told him that if we wanted to stay married, we had to separate our money."

They created a house account to pay their mutual bills, and each contributed equally to it. For the most part, this arrangement worked beautifully. Amy indulged in her love of kitchen accessories and black shoes outside of Andy's anxious eyeshot. Andy could invest in stocks, along with his political causes, which Amy would have nixed. Moreover, they educated their boys, paid for summer camps, maintained a nice home, and kept the property taxes and mortgage up to date. The trust issue faded into the background.

Complications returned after Amy lost her job at the public relations firm where she'd worked for ten years. The company's headquarters was moving out of Pittsburgh, and neither Amy nor Andy had any desire to leave their hometown. But for the first time in twenty years, Amy couldn't keep her side of their financial bargain. Now, in her midforties, she faced having to rely on Andy.

"I had been independent, and that had saved me more than once in this marriage," she confesses. "I love Andy, but sometimes we're very different. Also, I never want anyone to control me with money. My mother always made her own money, and I have made mine. That's just how I like it." She felt totally unprepared for what happened when she asked Andy to carry their expenses until she got another job.

"He loved being asked. He was happier than I'd seen him in years. It wasn't that he was just willing; he was eager.

I think that part of him really didn't feel appreciated or needed or something. Not only that; we started having the best sex we'd had in years. If I'd known it was going to be that way . . ." Her voice trails off, but then she adds, "No, I wouldn't change anything. I still like knowing it's my money and my life."

Only after Amy had to look to her husband to cover the bills did she realize that she'd actually paid a price in intimacy in exchange for her desire to be financially independent from him. By not mingling their money, they'd avoided the trust issue but inadvertently created another. Andy actually *wanted* Amy to depend on him. It gave him a sense of purpose. He used to joke all the time about how much Amy spent, but deep inside, he'd always felt a little inadequate because he didn't feel needed.

Many of us recognize the benefits—the freedom, self-esteem, and personal satisfaction—of economic independence in a marriage. But there are also the more urgent issues of control and autonomy. Like Amy, I also never seriously imagined a time when I wouldn't work. By the time I met Steve No. 1, I had been supporting myself for almost fifteen years. I made a nice salary. I owned my own home; I had no debt outside of a manageable mortgage. He made a better salary, had child support payments, also owned his apartment, and had a few stubborn IOUs that he was anxious to retire. A few months after we met, he suggested renting out his place and moving in with me so he could save enough to pay down his markers. Mindful of my grandmother's warnings about a man not wanting the cow if he already had its milk, I declined. "I only want to live together if we're getting married," I said. Two months and no engagement later, he moved in. (So much for the milk and the cow.)

Right from the start, I had two opposing sets of feelings about how my eventual husband dealt with our newly joint finances, which, rightly or wrongly, he probably interpreted as being about more than money. I delighted in his desire to control our cash and in the emotional freedom of not having to be the one to worry about the day-in, day-out financial demands of our lives. But new worries replaced my earlier ones. When he decided that he'd do his own investing, I fretted that he'd lose everything we'd saved; while he loved to gamble, the stock market looked like one big crapshoot to me. I took the little red cape off the wolf outside the door and spread it over my husband's shoulders. It wasn't that I didn't trust him in particular. I didn't trust *anyone* with my money—not even myself. But I also knew that he took pride in the research he conducted and the investments he made. I had to tread carefully.

I did what I had always done when I didn't want to come out directly and say something: I beat around the bush. I blathered on about how he didn't have the time, how the stock market was so tough, about how well my father's broker had done over the last five years. I did everything but say, "Hey, you're making me nervous!" But I didn't come straight out and ask him *not* to do the investing. I knew it was important to him, and frankly, I feared his response. I knew my doubts would anger him and make him feel disrespected, so I decided to trade silence for my husband's self-esteem. If I did this, I rationalized, he would love me more and never leave me.

But I couldn't keep my side of the bargain. Instead, I began to lob anxious zingers into the den, where he sat poring over big binders of investment information. I don't remember now how our stocks performed or whether we lost or made money. That's probably because it was less about the cash than about whether or not the marriage was going to flourish along with our IRA portfolio.

There are women, and I am one of them, who need to know that everything is going to be okay. Since I couldn't control the marriage, I went for the stocks. And when I felt my husband spinning away from me, I held on ever harder, even as doing so choked the life out of our relationship.

Second-guessing my husband's financial acumen certainly contributed to our marriage's slow strangulation. As my behavior alternated between the conciliatory Inner Stewardess approach and a desperate panic, I'm sure I drove my husband crazy. Steve is a perceptive man. He probably recognized that my anxiety sprang from my constitutional insecurity and consequent need to control. However, looking back, I now see how it must have felt to him—as though I was sending him the much more damning message that I didn't have faith in his judgment and his abilities as a provider. Money became the medium through which I exposed—to myself and to him—my doubts. As long as these doubts stay below the surface, most of us are content to leave them in the dark. It's hard looking at someone you love and realizing that you don't feel safe in his hands.

In a marriage, sometimes it's easier to focus on the financial concerns than the underlying emotional differences or wants. It's much less threatening to argue with your spouse about how he or she behaves with money than it is to take on some of the bigger issues: the lack of emotional trust, the desire for more intimacy, the need for recognition or simple attentiveness. Instead, these needs find monetary proxies in investment gambles, hidden financial stashes, financial withholding, and economic irresponsibility.

From his perspective as a psychotherapist and marriage counselor, Stephen Goldbart has seen the impact of money issues on relationships. He says that money itself rarely causes marital tensions, even if it is a common flashpoint. While people often admit that money problems cause fights in their marriages, they also say that deeper emotional issues are ultimately responsible for the end of their marriages. "It's not the money per se that causes fighting or even divorce," he says when I ask him if money arguments really end marriages. "But money has a lot to do with power and self-esteem. Whether you give it or not means you love me or don't love me. In the psyche of people today, it's hard for them to sort out these differences. Obviously money is a vehicle for the communication of how partners feel about each other. It signifies whether you esteem your spouse or whether you esteem yourself and whether you do or don't have power in and out of the marriage."

WOMEN AND MEN rarely differ when asked what they really want out of life. But a 2001 Yankelovich survey found that even when men and women had similar life priorities and financial goals, *how* they achieved both differed profoundly. While 85 percent of both sexes cited "family and love relationships" as their two top priorities in life, men were more willing to take bigger risks to support their dreams. Not too surprisingly, women categorized themselves as "bargain hunters" who were more concerned about retirement, debt, and "making it through the week."[5]

One of the biggest differences lies in the different approaches men and women take toward investing. Any financial adviser knows that women, on average, are more conservative investors than men (even though their track record is often better because they don't trade stocks as often and as quickly as men do). Why? When it comes down to it, women cite a lack of confidence and interest. Or, as the 2005 Merrill Lynch Investment Managers Survey put it, the reasons come down to "time and fear."[6] Among the participants in this survey, 60 percent of the women said they preferred to spend as little time as possible managing their investments, versus 49 percent of the men. The women who were surveyed didn't want to make investment decisions by themselves; they'd rather make them collaboratively with their husbands. These women felt reluctant about taking responsibility for a stock's performance, and 47 percent of them said they didn't feel they knew enough about investing, versus only 30 percent of the men.

In other words, women typically fear being the one in charge of the couple's investments. Sometimes this fear shows up disguised as indifference. Either way, this hesitancy shifts the burden to the husband, who, if he doesn't correctly understand his wife's tolerance for risk, can quickly find himself on contentious ground. A loss of money due to a poor investment signifies a loss of power for men. A woman will experience the same situation more emotionally, feeling that it threatens either her security or her children's futures. Clearly, men and women experience both reactions, but gender differences do tend to prevail.

These basic differences in male and female approaches to money can ignite power struggles that are easily exposed by even the smallest of incidents. Susan swears the beginning of the end of her marriage had to do with curtains. She wanted some. She'd just moved into her first truly grown-up home. Feeling a bit insecure about her own interior design abilities, she asked her friend Nancy, who had a very elegant and upscale decorating business, for help. The bedroom was particularly challenging. "Drapes," Nancy declared, waving her arm at the windows. "You need dramatic, fabulous drapes. And I know just the place to get them."

When Susan shared the price tag for these dramatic and fabulous drapes with her husband, John, he wondered if she had taken complete leave of her senses. "How much?" he asked in disbelief. After Susan repeated the sum, he told her, "That's more than I spent on my first car! I don't even want curtains."

"But that's what they cost!" she retorted, not knowing *what* she was talking about and digging into her position more out of a feeling of being denied than out of a desire for the drapes themselves. The issue had swiftly shifted from window treatments to who had the money veto and therefore who had the power in their marriage.

Susan tended to rationalize her spending by saying she was buying things for the house, not for herself. She liked to spend but hardly considered herself a shopaholic. John accused her of being in denial about how much money she actually went through. Susan thought John—who came from a more modest background—didn't appreciate her good taste. He thought she'd ignored his wishes for a much simpler decor (which she had, in fact, completely failed to register).

Susan felt misunderstood. John felt he'd married a woman who was not only deaf to his wishes but a total spend-thrift. While they wrestled about money on the surface, what was really at stake was their differing visions of the most intimate part of their lives. Cloaked in a disagreement over thirty-dollars-a-yard fabric lay fundamental differences— the kind that reveal themselves only when two people want to create two different lives out of one pot of money.

The writing was on the (naked) walls.

Stung by John's allegations about her spending habits,

Susan temporarily retreated into Inner Stewardess mode and tried to be who John wanted her to be. She bought pull-down shades.

But the damage was done. John lost his confidence in his wife's ability to restrain her spending. Susan decided John was both tacky and stingy. No shades could block out those feelings. John left within the year. They sold the big house and bought two smaller ones. The first thing Susan bought for her new bedroom? Drapes.

By then Susan's decorator friend, Nancy, was having her own issues with her husband, Henry. He'd wanted more kids (he had two from a previous marriage), but Nancy was having trouble conceiving. Three in vitro fertilization treatments later, the twins arrived. One had a hole in his heart and required immediate surgery. Nancy gave up her design business and became fully devoted to the kids. What time she had left over was spent transforming their home into a showcase. Henry gave her a chunk of money and told her, "Go with God."

She called in the contractors; she knocked down walls, redid the kitchen, and landscaped the yard. Then she decided they needed a bigger home.

They moved. Henry handed over the same-size sum as before. Nancy said that wouldn't even get the bathrooms done in the new place. Henry doubled it. Nancy looked at him. "Triple," he said. "That's all."

She called back the contractors, knocked down more walls, redid the kitchen, and landscaped the yard. She joined the PTA at her kids' school. She headed the school auction committee.

Henry joined a golf club.

Nancy put in a pool.

Henry played golf every weekend.

Nancy bought a Lexus SUV.

Henry went to Scotland with the guys to golf and drink.

Nancy added a large sapphire and diamond ring to her Christmas list.

Henry gave her the ring.

Henry gave up sex.

Nancy tried everything. Lingerie, trips. Sending the kids away to her parents. But after more than five years with no lovemaking, Nancy was beginning to think Henry was having an affair. Then she thought about having one. They'd been through couples counseling, during which the counselor had suggested that Henry might just be withholding sex out of a need to control something in his life. Nancy retorted, "Nonsense. Everything revolves around Henry's life." Henry looked at her wide-eyed and started to speak about what he saw as her unending appetite for his money but silenced himself halfway through the session. Nancy wanted to tell him that if she didn't feel so lonely, she might not spend so much. It all went half said. Eventually, they gave up on the therapist and instead retreated into a collegial companionship. Nancy, resigned, went back to gardening, and Henry golfed. One day, in the midst of a rotten cold, he moved into the guest room so he wouldn't keep

Nancy awake with his snoring. He never returned to their bed.

"Do you ever think of leaving?" I asked her one day as we walked along the beach near her home.

"Not really," she said. "He's a great father to the boys, and he is very nice to me—well, except for the love-life part."

I said nothing, as I was thinking about my own marriage. My husband was traveling constantly. When he was home, he retreated into his den or disappeared into the television set or napped as he tried to sleep off his incessant jet lag. As he pulled away, I became more and more accommodating, but all this did was make him back away more or snap at me. Clearly, this independent woman he'd married had turned into something unrecognizable.

We were four years into our marriage, and somewhere inside me I knew our problems were caused by something more than discordant time zones. The marriage wasn't working, and, at a certain level, I knew it. Indeed, as Nancy talked about her marriage, I remembered a scene from my own. My husband had just cut me down for some new carpeting I'd had installed in his absence. I recalled sitting on the kitchen counter, my feet in the sink, looking out the west-facing window and watching the sun set. I sat there, utterly defeated, and tried to figure out how many years it would be until my son was old enough to withstand a divorce. Fifteen. I reckoned I had to wait fifteen years before I could leave.

What, I wondered, kept us in these marriages?

For me, it was mostly the conviction that, having never had an intact family when I was growing up, I wanted to give my son what I had missed. For Nancy, it was probably the same. Indeed, in all the surveys that list reasons why people stay together, doing so for the sake of the kids always comes out on top.

But what about the lifestyles?

To be quite candid, neither Nancy nor I could have maintained ours if we got divorced. It took two incomes to pay for our homes and to be able to send our children to decent schools. Nancy depended totally on Henry for every cent she spent. She'd given up her business to take care of the kids. Even an excellent alimony and child-support arrangement wouldn't allow her to re-create her current life. I made a nice living, but a divorce would definitely mean a far less comfortable lifestyle. Were these considerations part of the equation? The part of me that shuns the material life scoffed. The rest of me wasn't so sure.

I had an incentive to stay in the marriage in part because I liked being able to write books for a living. Even though I was making as much money from writing as I had from my previous corporate job, the income came in spurts. My husband's steady checks meant there were no cash-deprivation moments. That meant I worried less. Then, there was that big payoff promise: It wasn't lost on either of us that when his company went public within a few years, he would be able to retire. I convinced myself (wrongly as it turned out) that if he didn't feel the pressures of having to work so hard, or even work at all, our marriage would turn around. Money wrapped itself around our problems. I thought that if we had enough of it, my husband would magically fall back in love with me because all the burdens he felt about being a provider would be relieved.

I never got the chance to find out. In the end, our problems had little to do with money. As my husband always said, we were better off as friends, not lovers. But money was a neat way to focus our differences without actually attacking the other person. As for Nancy, ten years on, she's still married to Henry. They settled in for the long haul. She loves him in a way she's become accustomed to. They still don't have sex.

MONEY CAN TRAP people in marriages. For most of history, marriages were really economic transactions between two people—one who had the right to create wealth, make money, and inherit property, and a partner who performed the unpaid work of the home. A man might live without a wife, but a wife cast out of a marriage would probably not survive. But it's not so clear today. Most two-income families live at a level that no one income can maintain. Experts divide on the reasons. Some say our spiraling appetites for material goods and resulting debt have tethered us to two paychecks. There's much to back up this argument. In 1960, the average American household had no credit cards. By 2004, every student entering college was bombarded with them. In

1960, kids wore inexpensive Levis. Maybe Wranglers. Now there are blue jeans boutiques where salespeople size up your parts and hand over the $150 jeans that are most likely to fit. Forty years ago, kids wore $6 Keds sneakers; today they clamor for Nike's $90 Air Jordans. For a generation that sang the praises of free love and communal simplicity, we've done a good job in leading the nation on a decades-long spending spree.

Harvard's Elizabeth Warren and her daughter, the attorney Amelia Warren Tyagi, don't deny materialism's impact on our rising levels of debt. But in their insightful book, *The Two-Income Trap,* they point out that something else has occurred. As women went to work and provided an additional income for their families, they began to use that money to buy homes and pay for their children's educations. The competition for these cornerstones of the emotional middle class's comfort zone has, in effect, created a bidding war. With two contributing incomes, the market for good housing in good school districts has gotten so competitive (hence so costly) that couples who succeed in buying a house find themselves trapped by their mortgages and education expenses. Warren and Tyagi note that a child growing up today is more likely to see his or her parents go bankrupt than get divorced. In the last twenty years, the number of women who have filed for bankruptcy has skyrocketed 662 percent.[7]

In a marriage, this level of debt not only yokes couples together economically but often does so in the very charged atmosphere of wanting to provide the best for their children. Emotionally, this situation cannot possibly become more fraught, given how much is at stake. Dual earning and household responsibilities also beg a level of equality between spouses that seldom exists in the way lives are actually lived. According to the Whirlpool study cited earlier, 88 percent of women still feel they handle the lion's share of home and child-care responsibilities.[8] More than once I've turned to my (very enlightened second) husband after a long day at the office, grocery bag or two on hip, and snapped, "I feel like I do everything in this house!" Which doesn't happen to be true. Well, not entirely.

Sometimes this setup brings out the worst in us. Karen, the unemployed magazine executive whose husband refused to get a better job when she was fired, tells me that she'd love to leave her husband. But they can't afford to separate. She offers that the only way out for her is if her husband dies. "He smokes, he has that big basketball-stomach thing that makes him a candidate for a heart attack, and he doesn't take care of himself. If he croaks, there's enough insurance to pay off the mortgage and to pay for the kids' schools."

Then there's Helen. For years, she had an excellent career as a powerful sales executive. During the go-go dot-com years, her husband, Don, became a paper millionaire and urged Helen to take a much-desired break. One daughter was in middle school, the other a freshman in high school, and Helen wanted to spend more time with them since they were growing up so fast. Her father was also ill, and she wanted to be around to supervise his medical care. When Helen's company was acquired by a major international concern, she had no desire to adjust to a new and very bureaucratic corporate culture. Yes, she and her husband agreed, it was a good time for her to stop working for a while.

Helen loved taking time off—which is how she looked at it. She didn't intend for it to be a permanent arrangement. She cooked, took yoga classes, ferried her father to doctors' offices. She figured she'd go back to work in a year or two, so she kept one foot in the corporate world through a consulting practice—more for mental insurance than for the income. Under the best of circumstances, Don was a challenging husband who demanded to know where she was and what she was doing all day. Helen wanted to have her own money so she could operate under his radar when she needed to. Also, Don tended to spend enormous sums of money impulsively—behavior that struck terror in Helen's heart. One day he came home with a Porsche Cayenne SUV; a week later, he announced he wanted to buy a second home. They were going to be rich, he figured, so why not? Helen shuddered each time the needle ticked off more mounting debt, but she kept quiet, partly out of a desire not to tangle with Don, but also out of denial. She simply didn't want to deal with it.

Then the tech bubble burst. Overnight, the value of Don's stock options plummeted. Their marriage swiftly followed suit. Don took out his frustration on Helen. She found a new job and went back to work to help support the family. But things went from bad to worse. Don wouldn't pick up his share of the household responsibilities, and Helen's new position required constant travel. One evening, while Helen was on a business trip, she got a call from her younger daughter, who was wondering if anyone was going to pick her up from soccer practice. Helen realized she'd had enough. She came home and asked for a separation.

They stayed separated for two years. Not because they hoped to reunite but because Don kept postponing a financial accounting, which, he said, they couldn't afford. They stayed in this unpleasant domestic limbo until Helen was called into her boss's office and told she was being let go in a corporate downsizing.

Initially, Don, who always rose to his best in a crisis, was very supportive. But a couple of weeks into her unemployment, he announced that he was ready for the divorce if she still wanted it. "This must be a mark of my mental instability," she cried to me on the phone. "I loathe this man, but do you know I was sadder than I've ever been when he said that? I've never felt so scared and alone. The guy's a nut, he's made my life miserable, and he stresses out our children. I've wanted this divorce for years, but all I could do was cry after that conversation. I just feel so alone. Like I have no one to fall back on now. Isn't that crazy?"

Helen wasn't nuts. Or at least not in any way many of us wouldn't understand. Even though she'd provided the main support for her family, she still craved the illusion of safety her marriage gave her. "If I really am honest," she concluded, "I have to admit that I didn't mind keeping things the way they were. I guess I was content to trade some misery for some security, even though I know that was just a fantasy, too."

I understood how she felt. There are times when, no matter how successful you've been at providing for yourself, you worry that you can't do it alone forever. That without someone—a parent, a boss, or a husband to whom you probably shouldn't be married—you will be too vulnerable and succumb to a lonely and destitute fate. The question is, what are we willing to trade to fulfill that fantasy? What is it worth to us? As my marriage started to crumble, I began to see the real cost of my membership in the emotional middle class; I was beginning to question the dues.

· 7 ·

THE DEATH OF THE
INNER STEWARDESS

ANTS. IT HAD BEEN THE ANTS THAT FINALLY SNAPPED the fragile threads holding my marriage together. There were thousands of them marching around the kitchen on their erratic, determined courses—on the counters, in the drawers, crawling across the refrigerator. It made sense; after all, Singapore sits a couple of very humid degrees above the equator. My husband pointed out somewhat tersely that he hadn't had them in the kitchen before my son and I arrived a couple of weeks earlier to join him. But then again, *nothing* was in the kitchen before we showed up. He ate out all the time.

I called an exterminator. Or at least I think it was an exterminator. In Singapore, people speak many languages, few of which were mine. The not-too-helpful man couldn't come for a few days anyway. I tried another number, then another language, growing increasingly frantic with each call; if I could just conquer the ants, I believed, everything else would magically get better. In my questionably rational mind, the inability to control my marriage's skid and rid the kitchen of pests had become one.

Every story has a turning point that, when passed, makes it impossible to view everyday, ordinary life with the same innocence or denial possible even a few moments earlier. Sometimes, events slide slowly, revolving around an invisible axis. One day we look up and everything looks and feels different. Other times, change arrives in seismic jerks. In an instant, familiar landscapes shift irrevocably. Those equatorial ants fell into this latter category. One moment, I battled and swatted at them on a hot and steamy December night, doing so with the furious conviction that my entire life depended on their eradication. A few minutes later, everything was uprooted.

"We need to talk," my husband said, ushering me into the sunken living room of the sublet apartment. I sat down on a rented (and hideous) black and gold brocade couch (which didn't bother my husband; his identity wasn't defined by what his sofa looked like) opposite the biggest television I'd ever seen (which also didn't bother him. Me? I hated a TV in the living room), a married woman with insect and relationship problems. By the time I stood up half an hour later, all my issues about the bugs, the sofa, and the TV were completely irrelevant. Nothing was going to save our marriage. In a single conversation my purpose, dreams, and expectations were shaken enough that they slipped off their hangers and hooks and dropped in a tangle to the floor. As I picked my way over these crumpled, familiar pieces of my life, I felt dizzy and disoriented. Two thoughts washed over me. The first was a kind of disbelief that this was happening. The other, almost simultaneous, was that destiny was doing for me what I couldn't do for myself.

Pushed through the threshold that I'd previously hung back from crossing, like it or not, I was about to enter into a world where I had neither parent, nor husband, nor employment to depend on. That vulnerability filled me with dread but also strangely elated me. Whatever was going to happen, I knew I was no longer prepared to trade myself for financial security. No amount of money was worth it. I stood in the doorway of the guest bedroom where I'd been sleeping and tried to focus. What was I supposed to do? Even though part of me instinctively realized this was, in fact, a positive development and probably paved the way for both of us to be much happier in our lives, at the time I didn't feel too good. I'd been focusing my energies on our marriage for so long that I'd lost sight of my own independent identity. That and the fact that suddenly my financial situation was anything but secure. I had—of my own choosing— handed over both to my husband when I entered into an agreement a few years earlier, the marital contract where we promised we'd go through thick and thin, raise our kids together, keep each other company, share emotional and physical intimacy. But of course there had been more than that involved. Buried in a subclause somewhere was that language about being taken care of. I thought that if I could just hold up my end of the bargain and do things to please—like killing a million ants—that someone would take care of me forever.

Suddenly, I was that someone.

I HAD JUST joined the ranks of women for whom Prince Charming had come and gone, and the statistics weren't pretty. In the 1980s, the sociologist Lenore Weitzman warned that when a woman got divorced, her standard of living dropped a jaw-dropping 73 percent.[1] (Although this statistic was later proven to be an exaggeration [it was actually 27 percent],[2] it captures the precipitous economic decline most divorced women face.) As Elizabeth Warren and Amelia Warren Tyagi point out, most mothers "tumble down the economic ladder" as a result of divorce, regardless of class.[3] In fact, "the drop is hardest for women in the middle and upper classes, since they have farther to fall." As a single mother, I was now more likely than any other group to file for bankruptcy, "more than the elderly, more than divorced men, more than minorities, and more than people living in poor neighborhoods." I was 50 percent more likely to go bust than I had been when I was married, and 150 percent more likely to wind up in bankruptcy court than any of my friends—married or single—who didn't have kids.[4] In fact, Warren and Tyagi predict that one in every six single mothers will go bankrupt by the end of the decade if things don't change.[5]

Even though I knew rationally and from experience that I had the ability to make a decent living, that knowledge didn't seem to alleviate the sense of doom I felt at having this huge emotional safety net snatched away. Some of these forebodings were financial, some social, and some neurotic. But the real body blow came from realizing just how fragile and tenuous that net turned out to be.

The truth is that I could have limited the repercussions of my sudden exile if I'd only been a little more interested or involved in our financial decision making. But I hadn't wanted to be bothered with money. I'd willingly turned a blind eye to managing it, and now I'd been sucker-punched by my own wishes. It's embarrassing to admit that. But it's true. Because I had consciously married someone who liked making, investing, and controlling the money, I didn't have to face my anxieties about it. I didn't have to follow our economic fortunes up and down or worry. I had drunk the cultural Kool-Aid that told me that having a husband meant social and fiscal security and that I wouldn't have to deal with my own financial well-being.

"The thing about money is that it's easy to ignore until you can't ignore it anymore," says Barbara Stanny, the author of *Prince Charming Isn't Coming*. "We have this fantasy that something's going to save us. Money feels so overwhelming and so confusing, but it seems that many women don't have the energy, the time, the skills, or the interest to do anything about it. That's why there's still that Prince Charming syndrome. I talk to my kids and their friends about this all the time. It's as true for younger women as it is for their mothers. And Prince Charming doesn't need to be a man; it can be work or an amorphous 'something.' There's this real rescue fantasy that is in our collective unconsciousness."

But what did I want to be rescued from? Uncertainty, certainly. Penury, of course. But in truth, at the end of the day, I wanted to be insulated from my own fears. I simply didn't trust myself to make the right decisions, and with such high stakes—my personal security and my son's—I was afraid to gamble. And because money is never just money, but instead is a stand-in for other things, ultimately, I didn't trust that I could take care of myself—not simply financially but emotionally.

"We all want something to stand between us and the terror of not knowing what's going to happen in the future," says the financial expert Pamela York Klainer. "Because of culture and family and history even the most able women still want to be taken care of and to believe there is somebody bigger and stronger than us." Klainer calls this the Oz Equation. "Remember that scene in *The Wizard of Oz* where the all-powerful person behind the screen turns out to be only this little shriveled-up elfin kind of man? Money, because it has a baseline ability to keep us safe, stands between us and powerlessness and uncertainty. When we reach a point where we take the veil away and say, 'I'm it, and it's my decisions that are driving my well-being,' everything changes. But we don't."

Instead of putting my faith in what was, after all, a proven ability to manage money (which I had done successfully for many companies I'd worked for), I had chosen to place it in a fantasy—the one where my husband would take care of my financial needs while all I had to do was keep him happy. In the end, the Inner Stewardess, with all her pleasing ways, hadn't accomplished any of her goals. She didn't save my marriage or my job, and, judging from the turn of events, she hadn't even kept me within the safety zone of the emotional middle class. All she'd done was distract me from being direct about what I wanted and why. In the end, not only had she proved useless; she'd actually led me into behavior that let me avoid taking responsibility for my own financial welfare.

The same thing happened with Sarah, a beautiful woman in her early forties. When her marriage ended, she realized she'd also given over everything to her husband. "I lost everything," she says. "I had done everything exactly as I thought it should be done, and when I left the marriage with three kids, one of whom has cerebral palsy, he offered me nothing." Sarah had married her college sweetheart and moved from her family straight to her husband. "Growing up, I got the impression that I would be taken care of by the things that my parents emphasized. I had cooking classes, sewing classes, ballet, dance, singing. At no point did I think I was going to get out of college and not be married. It didn't even occur to me. Even during college I thought I always needed to be with someone. I did think I would work, but I didn't even think it through. I didn't really believe I could support myself. It certainly never dawned on me that I could do this alone."

Indeed, Sarah did get married three months after she graduated and one month after Jesse, her fiancé, signed a lucrative baseball contract. Suddenly, they were millionaires. But Sarah never spent money on herself. She never questioned the small allowance she got from Jesse; all she really wanted was stability and safety for her kids. "My biggest financial regret is that I wasn't aware at all of where our finances were going in our marriage or that I had the power to say, 'No, I want to put the money in college accounts.' I never did that. I let him handle it. He had agents, and I assumed they had more responsible knowledge. My parents didn't do a great job at explaining that I could be responsible, too."

Sarah says that when she bought a few things, like a piano, she did so on a layaway plan because she didn't feel entitled to spend money. "I felt that since he was the one who was making the money, it was his and I would deal with what he allotted as a budget," she remembers. "Never once did I go out and spend on a shopping spree because I didn't feel like it was mine."

When the marriage ended, Sarah saw things differently. "I admit, my first thought was it's a good thing I'm beautiful, so I can marry someone rich. I'm talented and pretty, and I'll just find someone else."

But everything changed on the plane flying out from the East Coast with her kids back to California. "I had gone out and bought them all plane tickets. I had hired a moving company. It was my first big expenditure of money. It clicked. I got it that it was me or no one. When I got to where we were going to live, I immediately dropped the kids with my mom, went to the bank, and took half of what we had in our account—it was about $80,000. And that was what we lived on for four years until the divorce was over. At first, I wasn't going to do that because I thought, 'I don't want to get in trouble.' But then I realized, 'I don't have *anything*. I don't have access to money unless I do this.' Sure enough, within an hour of my withdrawal, Jesse had called the bank, and I wouldn't have gotten any money out. I put it in the bank next door. It was in that moment that the whole 'I'm-going-to-be-a-good-girl' was over. I've never looked back."

Sarah says that the idea of living a diminished lifestyle initially terrified her, and she was glad that she didn't know how hard it was going to be to take care of her family's basic needs. Indeed, despite all the money her ex-husband had, she had only managed to get enough for a down payment on a modest house near her mother. She's taken her ex-husband to court several times to try to get him to pay his child support, but he has dodged his obligations repeatedly. "The whole idea of taking care of everything scared me to death. But life happens, and it wasn't as scary as I thought. It's been hard work, but it wasn't what I thought it would be. With each new challenge, I became more present and more real. I was more me; I had more creative energy; I was more open to people; relationships meant more to me. All the things that I now define as life were more real to me because of that transition."

Sarah discovered that her marital cocoon had really been keeping her isolated from people. Without it, she had to connect with others. "The first time I realized how alone I had been was when I had to ask someone for help. I never had done that before. I couldn't pay for one of my kid's educational programs, and I asked a woman I knew with a lot of money if she could lend me a few hundred dollars. She was so happy to help me. And in that moment I thought, 'Wow, I've moved from this person who was living behind fences in this I-have-everything environment, this I-don't-need-anyone-else existence, to being connected with a lot of people.' When you've been humiliated or failed, you're humbled and you become more open to other people, and they are drawn to you to share their own not-so-positive experiences. So the plastic life of 'everyone-is-happy' goes away."

When I first met Sarah, she was way ahead of me on the path to clarity. She'd been divorced for five or six years. "Two years," she pronounced like an oracle. "In two years it will all look different." When I first heard her story, I was in the midst of negotiating my marital settlement. It was inconceivable to me that I would ever come to her point of view. But within a year, I began to understand what she meant. Money had begun to look like money, not love, not security, not a dream. It was something that I needed to live—as my friend Robin had said, nothing less, nothing more.

AS I SPOKE to younger women, they didn't seem to equate cash and emotional care in the way Sarah and I did. In fact, money seemed almost dissociated from their emotional lives. If they planned on marrying a man with money, as some of them said they did, they clearly saw the marriage as an economic transaction. Their agendas weren't as buried or disguised as it had been with women of my generation. This was clear the moment I met Emily Ann, a single woman in her midtwenties. She wears high heels effortlessly and walks lightly in them; her hair is straight and swingy and streaked with blond. She shares an apartment with three other young women as she pursues her dream of working in television news production. She has none of the illusions I had that her company is going to take care of her; she sees how easily people are hired and fired. "I don't have a lot of money, but I know I'm talented. I can always get a job. And I will always make sure I can pay my bills. Don't get me wrong; I want to get married, maybe even stop working when I have a family. But I don't think that turning into a Barbie doll is going to get me all those things. Being myself is. Being a go-along-to-get-along chick is not. What good is a nice house if you lose yourself getting it?"

When I ask Emily where she came by this wisdom, she says she watched her mother, who is now in her early fifties, wrestle with what Emily calls "a schitzy head" when it came to money. "I saw her suck up to her boss for years and years. I swear she almost had a nervous breakdown. She thought that if she just was a good foot soldier, then they would love her and promote her. She did one thing and talked another game, though. She always told me that I had to stick up for myself and make sure I was getting the same pay a guy would get and not to feel bad about asking for money. She couldn't do it, but she wanted me to."

Emily doesn't share her mother's guilt about her materialism, either. "My mom is an old hippie, really," she says. "She has all these issues about me being too commercialized and all that, but believe me, she likes her nice things. Not me. I love to shop. But so what? I also know I have to pay the bills. I came out of college with $19,000 in student loans. I *know* I have to pay the bills."

Emily knows that even when she finds a husband, he'll still probably be good for paying only half the freight. "Prince Charming may come along," she tells me, "but (a) that's the weight of Atlas to put on somebody's shoulders to expect that he's going to take care of stuff, and (b) that myth has never served anyone well." She feels she approaches money very differently from her mother. Her contract with money and a prospective spouse is much clearer. To her, she is responsible for creating her own security. She doesn't expect anyone or anything will take care of her. "You see a lot of unhappy people from that," she says. "In my peer group, there are a lot more women staying home with children because it's the backlash to the boomer generation. I think it's both a backlash and because they can. But of all my friends who are staying home who've recently had kids, the majority have kept one foot in the workplace because they know they don't want to give up control of their lives."

Emily's roommate Gia also doesn't seem overly concerned about money—but for different reasons. She fully
expects that a future spouse will take care of her financial
needs. In the meantime, her parents provide continual economic subsidies. Even though they aren't wealthy, they pay
Gia's share of the rent. As for everything else, Gia relies on
about ten credit cards, which she displays for me on their
kitchen counter, to fill the gap between her paycheck and
her passions for nice clothes and cosmetics. When I ask her
how she expects to pay off her balances, she says she doesn't
know. But being in debt doesn't bother her. She figures
something will happen to take care of it.

Gia's unrealistic approach to personal finance is not
uncommon. In an age when adult children regularly return
home after college due to an inability to afford a life as nice
as they had with their parents, this attitude is not unusual.
But what does surprise me is the degree to which neither the
Responsible Emilys nor the Dreamers like Gia are willing to
compromise who they are by exchanging parts of their identities or their independence for financial security. They feel
entitled to both.

Perhaps having watched their mothers' struggles, younger
women have decided that the bargain simply isn't worth it.
While these young women have no fewer material desires
or appetites than their mothers, they seem to approach
them without the guilt and the emotional associations many
baby-boom women have. Benefiting from earlier generations' experiences, they see clearly that brokering bits of

themselves for security or status won't get them what they want. It simply ensures they will lose part of themselves in the chase. They like money—they are, after all, a generation that has been assaulted since birth by commercial messages urging them to buy the latest trendy and branded merchandise—but they don't seem to have the same faith that money or economic security buys happiness.

"Certainly, we have an equation in society that money equals happiness," Juliet Schor observes as we talk. "We have the idea that money equals security, that it equals success— and that's connected to the happiness. Freedom, happiness, fulfillment—pretty much all of the key positive values of American culture, independence—all of them have a very strong link to money. Money is seen by many people as the mechanism for getting those things."

Yet in the past decade, scientists and psychologists have been investigating whether this money-equals-happiness equation holds true. They've found that there's a limit to just how much happiness cash can create. While the research clearly documents that people are happier if they live in wealthier rather than poorer countries, once the basics are covered, it turns out that money doesn't improve the chances of being happy.[6] This is true not only in the world's wealthiest nation, the United States, but also throughout Europe, Australia, and Japan.

David G. Myers, a psychology professor and happiness researcher, points out that "wealth is like health: Its utter absence breeds misery, but having it (or any circumstance we long for) doesn't guarantee happiness."[7] He notes that although Americans' buying power has more than doubled since the 1950s, according to data from the National Opinion Research Center, "the average American's reported happiness has remained almost unchanged. Such findings lob a bombshell at modern materialism. Indeed," he continues, "if we can judge from statistics—a doubled divorce rate, more-than-doubled teen suicide, and mushrooming depression—contemporary Americans seem to be more often miserable." This state of being (also true for Europeans, Australians, and Japanese) is at serious odds with the other messages we get in our consumer society—messages that promise us that if we have the money to buy any given product, our happiness and fulfillment will be complete. Instead, quite the reverse turns out to be true.

"Enduring happiness doesn't come from financial success," concludes Myers. Indeed, the American Psychological Association categorically states that psychological research shows that "people who buy into the messages of consumer culture report *lower* personal well-being."[8] According to research by the psychologist Tim Kasser, "individuals who say that goals for money, image, and popularity are relatively important to them also report less satisfaction in life, fewer experiences of pleasant emotions, and more depression and anxiety."[9] These results hold true for people of various ages and in nations around the world.

"That's because money stands in symbolically for love," Pamela York Klainer reiterates as we discuss these findings.

"Let's say that I've been a pretty absent partner, and I go and buy a big holiday gift. Many people use money as a way of making up for what they haven't done. It also stands in for power and intelligence, and ambition." Klainer points out that our lives are very busy, and they move very quickly. "To develop an internal sense of what's good and what we value is a lot of internal reflection and a lot of work," she says. "What do you think is important in life? What do you want to achieve? What values do you want to transmit to your kids? Many people either don't do or don't know how to do that kind of internal work, so they let money stand in as the measure. If I can afford to buy a nice car and live in a nice neighborhood and have a lot of electronic toys and take the family on some great vacations, then I am successful. Well, maybe yes and maybe no. But we let money stand in because it's tangible and it's easy."

THIS IS THE point in my story where I'd love to say I had the epiphany about what money meant to me and that once I understood how I was asking it to buy something it couldn't, everything changed. But nothing of the sort happened. The last thing a newly single mother in the midst of negotiating a child-support agreement wants to hear is that she should substitute insight for cash. But the fog did lift long enough for me to glimpse what I thought was going to ensure my happiness might actually be standing in the way if I didn't start looking beyond it.

Two things were clear: I needed money. Absolutely. But what I definitely could no longer afford was an indirect, somewhat coy, and extremely emotional relationship with money. It was time to separate what a dollar could buy emotionally from what it purchased at the grocery store. There were emotional needs and material ones, and I wasn't going to be able to distinguish between them if I didn't face the fact that I could no longer afford to play the "Oh, I don't talk about money" game or pretend that money wasn't important to me. I was going to have to own up to my material desires and make some peace with them.

This point was made humiliatingly clear to me one night during a support-group meeting where I'd gone for some help in coping with my divorce. There were eight to ten well-heeled men and women, all of them a little older than I. They seemed to have been around the block a couple of times, and I leaned on their experience and the smarts that resulted from it. I was in the middle of negotiations with my soon-to-be ex-husband about child support, and I turned to the group in tears. "I have to get money for my son so he can have opportunities," I sniffled when it was my turn to speak. There was silence for a moment, and in that instant I felt completely understood, safe in their pity for me.

"Bullshit," barked a smartly dressed woman. "Stop hiding behind your child. You want a nice life for yourself, too. There's nothing wrong with that. Just come straight out and say it, though. You have to know that's what's driving your train here. Then you can have some control over where that train is going." My face began to burn with embarrassment.

"And you know what?" she continued. "If you don't come clean, your ex-husband's going to see how full of it you are, and it's going to hurt you financially in the long run." My vanity smarted under the sharp smack of the truth. My husband had frequently accused me of being disingenuous about my money wants. I'd always found a way to hide them behind everyone else's needs and welfare, or so I thought. Now even a total stranger could see that I didn't really want to take responsibility for my relationship with money.

I don't know what would have happened if that woman hadn't delivered such a blunt wake-up call. My hunch is that I wouldn't have been able to negotiate a financial settlement as cleanly and clearly as I eventually did. The negotiating process sure didn't feel comfortable, but my ex-husband appreciated my candor about my needs and wants, which made the whole nasty, sad business of putting a price on my life a little bit easier. Removing the emotional part from the compensation discussion also let me see that he had been very unhappy about the whole proceeding himself. Ultimately, it wasn't his fault that he loved me like a friend instead of a wife, and it wasn't my fault either. And if I hadn't been able to divorce the money from the emotion, I never would have been able to see his sorrow.

A few weeks after that evening, I had lunch with a woman named Angie. I'd gone back to work, where, in the process, we'd come across each other professionally. She swore we'd gone to high school together. She turned out to be right, but I would have put good money on the fact that I'd never seen her before in my life. She was tall (even without stiletto heels). Her expensively cut hair was blond-blondblond, and only the diamond on her left hand eclipsed the dazzling prominence of her breasts. This one I would have remembered. No one in my high school came remotely close to being so glamorous. Wendy MacAver came to school one day in the eighth grade sporting a Gucci handbag, but the rest of us were pretty run-of-the-mill, fairly grungy 1970s-era teens.

"I know, I look different," she said over our ladies' lunch at a fashionable restaurant. "But why not?" Angie was a take-charge type and immediately realized she had good, raw material sitting in front of her. "First thing you need to do," she commanded as I told her I was about to get divorced, "is call these five lawyers." She whipped out a leather-encased note pad and scribbled down the names.

"But I already have someone," I said, mentioning the name of my attorney.

"Oh," she snapped. "That one will just bleed you dry and not do what you want," she said (with what turned out to be astonishing accuracy). It seems I had hired a prominent lawyer who, unbeknownst to me, was famous for nasty theatrics. While I was very clear about what I wanted (which included going back to work and supporting myself), we were disagreeing radically about his proposed tactics. He wanted to do things like ambush my husband at the airport with divorce papers when he came to visit my son. I simply wanted to make a fair settlement.

"My husband will do the right thing, I'm sure," I told Angie as I felt my confidence draining away.

"Helloooo," she responded incredulously. "We're talking about a man who moved you to Singapore only to divorce you, honey. Do you think he's going to be fair? But don't use your lawyer—these guys are the best," she said, handing me the names and phone numbers. "Here's what you do. You make an appointment with each one; then your husband won't be able to use any of them—conflict of interest!" She flashed a satisfied smile. "Hey, it worked for me!"

I marveled at her strategy. Her cold, surgical skill. Her ability to know what she wanted (money and lots of it) without ambivalence and the fact that she was not going to let anything—or anyone—get in the way of her having it.

Was this what I had to do to secure my future? I made an appointment with the first attorney on Angie's list. He charged me $500 for the forty-seven minutes it took to meet him and tell him what I wanted. He told me that I sounded reasonable, that my soon-to-be ex sounded reasonable, and to try and work it out without hiring someone at his level. Maybe he was being nice. Maybe he didn't sense a lot of money in taking me on as a client. Either way, I walked out of his office across the polished marble lobby, crumbled up the list, and tossed it in the nearest trash can.

In the end, I asked for what I thought was fair in simple and direct terms. My husband countered with what he thought made sense. We weren't far apart. We both took responsibility for what happened in our marriage. He did the right thing by our son and by me. He was smart enough to know that while money couldn't buy love, an equitable arrangement could purchase emotional freedom.

As a freshly minted divorcée, I started out with a margin of financial stability—not enough that I didn't have to go back to work, but enough so that I was in no danger of the power company turning off the lights. But this cushion did little to assuage my pervasive anxieties about landing in the poorhouse. I began waking up in a sweat and tossing around, obsessing about how I was going to pay this bill or afford that repair. I started a list of catastrophic "what-ifs." Even I could see that the worry–probability of disaster ratio was way off. Emotions fueled my worries, and I simply couldn't get a handle on them.

"I have a theory about this," the money expert Barbara Stanny tells me when I relate this story. "It's not about money; it's about power. The reason women are reluctant to directly face money has nothing to do with money itself but everything to do with power. Taking financial responsibility and becoming financially independent is a rite of passage into our power. I really do believe that power demands that we become responsible adults—the ultimate authority in our lives—and money enables us to do that. I think we're scared of the power. Power demands that we stand up and think and act for ourselves. It demands that we take up space, that we value ourselves. With power comes responsibility and visibility."

"But I've always paid my own way," I protest at first. "It can't be about power. I'm not afraid of that."

Later, as I contemplate Stanny's remarks, I realize she may be on to something. Even though I'd been self-supporting, I'd never equated money with power. When I made more than someone I dated, I may have downplayed that fact because I was afraid that I'd be less appealing if I didn't appear to "need" the man. But what did that have to do with power? Secretly, I may have felt capable, but powerful? No.

But money *is* power. Men know that. Women know it, too, but we are reluctant to claim it for fear of its power to divide us. Yet reluctant or not, women will ultimately have more money than men. In the last decade alone, more than $8 trillion transferred to a younger generation—more than 55 percent of which went to women.[10] That same percentage of employed women bring in half of their household incomes, and one out of four married women outearn their spouses. So why are women reluctant to claim the emotional power that comes with the economic one?[11]

For Klainer, this is an essential question. "For years, women expected to go from their fathers' homes to their husbands' homes. Part of that expectation involved being taken care of and its corollary that there is somebody bigger and stronger than me. I think when we reach a point where we take the veil away and say, 'I'm it, and it's my decisions that are driving my well-being,' everything changes."

Indeed, I had arrived at just that place. It had taken a jarring divorce for me to see that I'd misjudged the power of the bargain I had made years earlier—the one that promised that if I were a good girl, everything would work out fine. Economic security has nothing to do with conciliating, pleasing behavior. I could have killed all the ants in Asia, and my husband would still have asked me to go home.

It was time to have some faith in my own evident abilities. Prince Charming had left the building.

· 8 ·

EGOCIDE
(OR DOWNWARD MOBILITY)

THIRTY YEARS AFTER SHE'D GONE TO HER GRAVE, MY grandmother had come to my rescue. Some years earlier, I'd taken her advice and started my own *knipple*. Ever since, I'd socked away a hundred dollars here, a few hundred dollars there. It didn't amount to much—and I had completely forgotten all about it until a few months after I returned to the States. But it was a bank account my husband knew nothing about, and something about that gave me a real boost. By the time I landed in San Francisco, partly buoyed by an unexpected royalty check from my publisher, the account was up to about $8,000. Not retirement money, granted. Still, it was mine. Suddenly, I was back in the business of making independent choices.

For the first time in a long while, I felt some sense of personal power. My stash was going to do more than rent me an apartment, buy me a car or some decent job-interview clothes; it was also going to give me some independence with which to start my life over. Even though I was negotiating for help from my husband, now there was not as much need for an emotional or financial bailout. I had what I needed to re-create my life.

I flattered myself that my husband had misunderstood me; I really didn't need much. I'd never spent more than $1,500 for a car. (Okay, that was before I had a child.) And hadn't I been the one who had lived in that crash-pad flat in the Mission District? I'd been without many resources before; I could definitely do this.

With confidence, I hoisted myself off my friend Sue's couch, where I'd been lying and listening to Dvořák's lugubrious *Nocturne for Strings* over and over and over again, and made my way to a local car dealer. The nice man there was happy to show me several used cars, but the only ones I could afford looked like they would end up back on the lot within the year.

Then I went to a realtor's office. It was the middle of the dot-com boom in what was already one of the country's most expensive housing markets. A dark two-bedroom shoe box on the ground floor in a dicey neighborhood at the end of a streetcar line cost $2,500 a month.

I enrolled my son in a sweet hippy preschool that had a goat, a bunch of chickens, and two wooly sheep.

Tuition? $5,000.

So much for my stash. I went back to the couch.

Never had money's power felt more limited. My *knipple*

certainly hadn't come close to helping me pick up where my old lifestyle had left off. Somewhere between the old days of driving an orange 1970 Datsun 310 with the rusted-out floor and my current residence on Sue's sofa, my lifestyle expectations had undergone some definite changes. What I defined as necessary had increased in such small increments over the years that I hadn't noticed the steady uptick. Now I was facing the equivalent of sticker shock for what I'd come to call my normal life. Having earned my membership in the emotional middle class, I started to see that it wasn't going to be so kind as I slipped off down the back side of the mountain.

Something was going to have to give.

I sat down to take a good square look at my needs and wants, my envies and appetites. On a yellow legal pad, I listed all the things I thought I required and what it would cost each month to maintain them: home, health insurance, car, and day care. I totaled up the columns. Then I retotaled them. I rechecked each number, each line. Nope, no mistakes. I started crossing things out. With each swipe of the pen, another piece of what I'd come to expect as "necessary" fell away.

It wasn't the loss of a nice home or some new clothes or a decent car that scared me as much as it was the vulnerability I felt each time I drew a line across the page. I'd spent years aspiring to one life, and now—item by item—I felt I was dismantling not just a life but my very self. I was committing a kind of egocide.

For years I had managed to hide my material side under

the skirts of my perceived needs. In doing so, I disguised and diminished—mostly to myself—just how much I had become invested in the trappings of my outer life: how I looked, how my home looked. I'd spent an enormous amount of time and energy and money over many, many years fine-tuning and burnishing this part of me until it reflected precisely the image I wanted the world to see. I depended as much on my material side to define me as any job I'd ever had or any "Mrs." I'd ever put in front of my name.

In this pursuit, I was a poster child for my time. "We're living in a time in which the consumer norms in our peer group escalated very rapidly," Juliet Schor explains as we discuss why perfectly sensible people become captivated by material goods and strive to obey the siren call of the six-burner commercial stove. "This escalation comes from a combination of things. We've become a consumer society overflowing with advertising and marketing. Income distribution changed, with a lot more income flowing to the top 20 percent of people. And the growing importance of consumer goods and the mass media has made that top 20 percent the aspirational target for the other 80 percent." Schor neatly sketches the partnership between income and aspiration and observes that luxury has replaced comfort. Luxury has become a *need*. Prodded by prodigious advertising, people consume in accordance with their aspirations, rather than their wallets. That's how we've become a nation, says Schor, where the average personal credit card debt hovers between $8,000 and $9,000 and, on average, Americans save somewhere around 1 percent of our wages—less than the percentage in any other industrialized nation.

"We're really social creatures when it comes to consuming," she continues. "Part of why you want the six-burner stove is that so many people around you are getting them. That four-burner sitting there in your kitchen seems so inadequate because a stove isn't just a stove but an intensely symbolic item. I mean, how often are you going to use all six burners? But we want it because of all the social validation we get when people come in and see it." She sympathizes with those of us for whom a double oven represents the Holy Grail of homemaking and even laughs a bit at her own temptations. "I think it's very difficult to buck the trend of rapidly escalating consumer norms," she concludes kindly.

I feel a bit exposed after this conversation. My home had definitely been the canvas on which I painted the picture I wanted of my life. My ego was certainly involved in even the smallest purchases, like the blue glass drawer pulls I'd found at a flea market. I had tried to assemble a kind of perfection that would validate me, reflect my uniqueness, and let the world see I was tasteful, warm, and embracing. I wasn't simply building a home that mirrored who I was, I was also taking my income and polishing it.

In this pursuit I had plenty of company. With more than four out of five of all purchasing decisions being made by women, it's not surprising that home-furnishing marketers profit when we conflate our identities with our possessions.[1]

This material form of self-expression extends beyond

homes or home furnishings to consumer electronics, clothes, shoes, and all kinds of luxury items. We buy a piece of the aspirational dream with each snap of the credit card. We do it for comfort, for luxury, for ease. The very act of purchasing releases anxiety for most of us, while creating a sense of control and instant pleasure. But we also shop to sample a taste of what it must feel like to belong to the exclusive club of those for whom money doesn't matter. Most of us spend so much of our lives worrying about money and making ends meet that it feels like fair compensation to buy a little bit of fantasy from time to time. While this is equally true for men, women are the object of the marketers' focus simply because we purchase so much more than men do. Incessant advertising, catalogs, and online sites keep our appetites continually stimulated, leaving us with a low-level hunger that only more purchases seem to satisfy.

"I have a champagne-taste thing going on," admits Deanna, a single woman in her early forties. "That's one of the reasons I got into credit card debt. If I don't feel good, I'm going to the mall. I'm just going to buy myself something pretty. Retail therapy. Worry about it later. They're going to give me credit? Well, okeydokey."

Deanna, like many of her contemporaries, received her first credit card in the mail when she entered college. She didn't think twice about using it. She immediately fell behind in her payments. Then, when she turned twenty, a drunk driver killed her father, and she and her mother spent two years in court suing the driver of the car. By the time Deanna was twenty-two, she was $40,000 in debt. But the legal case ended with a substantial financial gain for Deanna. After paying off her credit cards, she went on a wild and extended shopping spree.

"That first couple of years I was very well dressed," she confesses. "After I paid my debts, I had a buffer of $30,000 dollars in my bank account, and I was also working. But there was no one there to say, 'You should be putting this money somewhere.' I did go talk to a friend once who was in investment banking, but never did anything about it. That thirty grand lasted five years, and then it was gone. When I realized I'd gone through it all and more, I felt ashamed. It was blood money; it was something I was supposed to have something to show for—but I had nothing."

Jean Chatzky, the financial editor of the *Today* show, tells me she isn't surprised that Deanna didn't know how to do anything other than spend. She'd had more than twenty years of consumer credit with which to channel her desires. "It's even more true today," says Chatzky. "More money is being placed in the hands of younger people sooner than it was in previous generations because they are being given credit cards and student loans. I think this makes them both more and less comfortable with big sums of money. They are more comfortable spending it, but to a lot of them, they think it's not real. They call it 'Monopoly' money. The average college student graduates with $3,000 to $4,000 in credit card debt plus $17,000 in student loans. And the default rate is high and continues to grow."

Women are outgunned. With multibillion-dollar marketing budgets urging women to buy, buy, buy in order to enhance their lives, impress their friends, and express their inner beings, it's difficult to push back against the consuming culture.

"Put all those microlessons together, and what they make you want is this perfect life," Chatzky observes. "In order to have it, you need to have the big house and two cars and gorgeous appointments and all those things that the middle class has locked itself into spending all of its disposable income on." We've been straightjacketed into spending like this because our identities have become fused with our purchases. Pulling back feels like a diminishment of our life possibilities.

When Deanna realized she had frittered away her father's inheritance, she felt so terrible about herself that she had to pull back. The damage was so severe that it took her four years to free herself from her creditors. "I consider myself middle-class, which doesn't mean a whole lot," she says. "Now there's a certain level that is comfortable for me. I don't have to be a millionaire, but I do want to keep myself comfortable, which means having an income, not having to worry about bills being paid, having a home that feels comfortable, not having to worry about creditors calling."

Deanna had to grieve the loss of the idea of financial salvation. "I thought I was going to have someone in my life to protect and guide me. And that's what money represents for me: safety and protection." The turning point came for her when she attended a two-weekend financial workshop.

Deanna had decided that she was going to tell the people in her group how it took her four years to get the creditors off her back and another six years to get out of debt entirely. She was determined that it wouldn't happen again.

When Deanna left the workshop, she says, she felt very exposed. "These were things people don't talk about. We know more about friends and relationships than financial things. We've been set up societally, but at the same time it's our responsibility." Opening up and talking about money allowed Deanna to feel she wasn't any more inadequate about money than anyone else. This gave her a sense of confidence that blossomed into independent power as she began to learn how to manage the money she had. "I feel stronger; I'm not afraid of what will happen. I don't need someone to come and save me."

But she admits that she still resists being responsible. She resents that she can no longer indulge in binge shopping. "I know I have to stay on top of it; otherwise, I'm not safe," she says with a sigh. "Being responsible with money is like my protector. My financial management is my husband. There isn't a living, breathing person who's going to make sure I'm okay. Instead of my dream man, I have financial responsibility to make me feel good about myself. Sometimes I feel great about it, but sometimes it pisses me off and I get so sad."

FOLLOWING MY DIVORCE, as I faced my own finite resources, I began my steady march in the direction of downward mobility. That material ego I'd enjoyed was no longer affordable. I had to revisit my definition of an acceptable lifestyle. I had to revisit just about everything. Overwhelmed, I fell into a depression.

One day, after dropping off my son at school, I retreated back to bed in order to nurse a case of temporary emotional paralysis. As I contemplated my options—or rather the lack of them—an apparition appeared before me. It was Mrs. Beatty, my next-door neighbor when I was in elementary school. She'd been the only divorcée in my small town on the Long Island Sound. No one got divorced in 1962, or so it seemed, so she became the standard-bearer for what divorce looked like. And it didn't look pretty. Mrs. Beatty may have been a talented woodblock artist, but she was one unhappy divorcée. Unhappy and lonely and up to her knees in sadness. Her husband had left her and the three rather feral Beatty kids for someone he worked with in "the City." The household fell into such a slovenly state of disrepair that when it burned down one afternoon, people whispered that it must have spontaneously combusted out of the dire need to be cleaned. Mrs. Beatty's life had definitely run off the rails after Mr. Beatty left.

As her kind but doomed face floated in front of me, I quietly realized that becoming Mrs. Beatty was a decision, not a fate. I had a choice about how I lived my life. I enjoyed opportunities that weren't available to most women of Mrs. Beatty's generation. Although I had followed her path somewhat by willingly bartering away bits of my personal power, authority, and integrity for what turned out to be fictitious stability, it was still completely within my power to make my own money and take care of my son. I had a choice about what I let money stand for emotionally. I'd given it the power to take care of me. And now that I saw I was mistaken, I had the power to take care of myself.

I began to reclaim some confidence. Hadn't I always made a decent living? I might not be able to afford my old life, but it was my decision whether or not I wanted to make that fact a misery. Mrs. Beatty, living as she did and when she did, had neither the options nor experience I'd enjoyed. From where I sat, it sure looked like a better bet to depend on my inner abilities than on an outer safety net. I was unwilling to ever again let myself feel as vulnerable as Mrs. Beatty—even if it meant sacrificing what I thought my lifestyle should be. What did a nice house matter if I had to pay for it by mortgaging myself?

Over the next few weeks, I began to feel more and more clearheaded. The rescue fantasy I'd held on to for most of my life started to dissolve. As it did, I realized that there was something comforting in this new, less emotionally loaded approach to money. Having less of it certainly meant I had fewer options, but strangely, that comforted me. I'd always wondered why puppies calm down when they're cooped up in their crates, but now I experienced the fiscal equivalent. When I would start to dream about buying an adorable little Victorian home, I would quickly realize I'd be lucky to have any home at all. I had faced a life-changing choice. Either I could be Mrs. Beatty, stuck mourning and moaning about the life and the dreams I had lost, or I could get off my duff and deal calmly and clearly with the cards I'd been dealt.

A realistic reckoning with money had revealed that my future happiness didn't depend on it. I had other resources—such as time—that were more valuable. It's as if my money and my mortality had become finite simultaneously. When I was young and immortal, I spent (or looked forward to spending) endless sums on my happiness. Then, the road narrowed. And now, what I truly couldn't afford was to put my faith in the old props to comfort and ego. It simply wasn't an option. And that was okay with me.

SARAH, THE FORMER wife of a baseball player, recalls a similar experience. "After a year and a half spent suing my husband in court, I finally got $200,000 out of him, and I turned around and put it all on a down payment for my house. My house is a cabin, not a castle. I would love a new kitchen, and I would love heat, and I would love insulation. But I'm really working on saying, 'Life is passing me by while I want all this stuff. I'm here, I'm here now, the kids are here now, and working so hard for something else is like kissing your life goodbye.' It's always on a platter out in front of you, but it's nothing you're eating at the time.

"I will consider myself completely successful if I can put my kids through college, even if it costs this whole house," she says. "I don't care if I have to sell it to pay off the loans; I will still feel I have completely succeeded. To me, now, the house is a vehicle. It's supported us. I trust that once the kids have gone to school, I will still be capable and able to take care of myself."

Much of Sarah's identity and how she valued herself used to rest on being a perfect mother with a perfect home. But with her three kids, a mortgage, and erratic child support payments, that quickly went out the window. After her divorce, she supported her family through substitute teaching. But she also set up a support network for parents of kids with cerebral palsy and spent up to twenty hours a week working for free, donating her time to this effort. "I was raised with a lot of community service. Social consciousness was engrained in us. That really affected my relationship with money because you didn't want to be selfish. If you had too much, you needed to give it away and put other people first. It all fell into not wanting to think about money because I grew up being told that only selfish, nonspiritual, uncaring people thought about money. I am just realizing now how much of my ego was caught up in all that."

After finding a way to support herself, Sarah realized how much it was costing her to give away her time for free. Yet she felt caught between the values of her childhood, which emphasized the need to place others' welfare first, and her own dawning belief that she deserved to be well compensated. "I still have this wrestling match with money that I'm trying to overcome because I am tired of being short at the end of every month because I don't charge for what I do."

Sarah's fight between the part of her that is truly generous, her selfless self-image, and her need for cash has been painful and exhausting, but it ultimately made her priorities very clear. "On the one hand, I'm stressed out, working all the time, taking on projects I don't want to do just to pay for my kids' things. But on the other hand, I wonder, 'What about me?' There's too much stress. I'm unable to keep in survival mode."

One day Sarah woke up with a headache. It didn't go away for two months. She was forced to take a step backward and see the price she would continue to pay if she didn't reorder her priorities. "I woke up one day and said, 'I'm losing me again just as I did in the marriage, where it became all about creating the life my kids needed to the point where I'm burned out. And at the bottom it's all about finances." Sarah realized that she couldn't afford to be the person she thought she should be. But it was so hard to let go of her community service work. "I got sick. I got those debilitating headaches because there was no other acceptable way out for me. I had to physically break down—there is no stopping in my life unless my body stops. When you lose everything like I did, you go into survival mode. Your brain switches over. You say to yourself, 'Never again. I will never put my kids through this again,' so you work harder and harder, and then you get to a point where you say, 'I'm depressed; I'm not happy; I'm finding no time for myself because I am taking all these other things on.' And then you look at your relationship with money and say, 'Okay, is money more important than *me*?'"

It took this physical breakdown for Sarah to realize that she could no longer afford to be "hands off" about money. She had to squarely face and embrace her material side and her material needs.

She could literally no longer afford the gratification she received from her uncompensated nurturing work. As a woman, she was sacrificing more than money, more than time. With every hour spent at work, she lost one with her children. With every hour she freely spent helping other mothers with their ill sons or daughters, she sacrificed income needed for her own. With each choice she offered up her dreams and hopes, her identity and her ego. Caught between two value systems and two sets of standards for what she wanted out of life, she was forced to create a balance, which she did by directly facing her money responsibilities while recognizing that her true wealth lay in her relationship with her family. The payoff has been profound. "I still don't want to make money for its own sake, but I'm also not willing to undervalue myself and my efforts anymore. My kids see this. They understand, as I didn't at their age, that a lot of their friends who have gorgeous homes also have parents who hate what they do even if they make a lot of money doing what they hate. I'm not willing to go there. They're not willing to go there. They want to be successful but only at something they like." Sarah feels she's finally achieved a balanced view of money. "When I first moved here, I was the poorest person in my community. It was embarrassing, but now I have a different standard by which I judge my life and worth."

. . .

WHEN SOMETHING IS taken away and we feel powerless, we can respond with resignation, acceptance, or stoicism. We can cry, get angry—even vengeful. In my case, every time I wanted to do something or buy something and realized I could no longer afford it, all those emotions washed over me, with a good dash of envy mixed in. As I neared the final negotiations for my divorce, every emotion I ever experienced about money swirled around my meetings with the mediator.

Everyone's divorce is different. But each requires us to put a price on our lives. That means that someone has to assign a value to something that the other spouse has just said they don't want anymore. It's a kind of paradox, one that requires a strong sense of inner worth to lay claim to an outer one.

But I knew one thing for sure: I genuinely wanted to be happy more than I wanted to be rich. I couldn't afford to be envious or spiteful or indirect. To negotiate for my future, I had to relegate all those old money-related behaviors to the sidelines if not permanently exile them. There was something money could buy in my divorce settlement—and that was good feelings. Not his at the expense of mine, or mine at the expense of his. Instead, we were going to have to find a compromise between money as power and money as connection. We were going to have to balance the imperatives of two systems to come up with one workable financial solution.

Above all else, my husband and I had a son in common. I had watched enough people scorch enough earth in divorces to know that all anyone got out of them was ash. Using money as a weapon has long-term repercussions, and neither of us wanted to live with the years of resentment involved. But that meant I was going to have to be completely honest about what I needed—not what I wanted.

Out came the legal pad again. I drew up a detailed budget. I wrote down what I estimated our living expenses would be—average, responsible expenses. I wrote down what I thought I could earn annually. Then, assessing the gap, I asked my husband to contribute toward closing it. Because I had been able to separate out my emotional needs from my financial ones, our negotiations were rational and calm, and we swiftly and very amicably worked out a settlement. I didn't get everything I wanted, and neither did he. But in the end, he felt good, and I felt good. We put a higher value on long-term friendship than we did on short-term economic gain.

The only moment of doubt occurred when I saw the final papers. The company for which my husband had worked for twenty-five years had indeed gone public during the course of our divorce (but after our negotiations), making my husband a genuinely wealthy man. When I saw how much he was now worth, I was stunned. I turned to my attorney and gasped, "Diana! What should I do?"

She looked at me, smiled flatly, and firmly instructed, "Sign the papers. You have what you need, along with something even more valuable than alimony. You have a good relationship with your ex. That's worth more than all his options put together."

She was right. And, after one last huge sigh, I signed the agreement.

IT DIDN'T HAVE to work out that way. If I'd let revenge or greed call the shots, if I'd been unable to let go of my dreams of a certain kind of house and a certain kind of life, I probably would have acted in a way that would have cost me for years. I'd watched as the fallout from angry, unfair settlements ate at both men and women years after they'd divorced. One man I knew, John, bitterly railed against his ex-wife, charging that he'd been "taken to the cleaners" (never mind he was an alcoholic with a roving eye who couldn't keep his pants zipped). He resented her so much that he took his fury out on his kids when they went to college. He told them to ask their mother for the money (she'd blown it years earlier) and never gave them a dime. But in the end, John lost much more than money. To this day, his kids resent their father and avoid having anything to do with him.

Another woman, Mary Beth, made the mistake of not killing off her Inner Stewardess before heading to divorce court. If she acted kindly during the proceedings, she reasoned, her husband would realize how wonderful she was and come back to her. This misguided strategy led to an even more lopsided financial settlement. She lost her home, her health insurance, and now, in her late fifties, has gone to work at Macy's to make ends meet.

I had negotiated my settlement and bought a small home. My son went off to his woolly sheep every day. I downgraded my panic about money to responsible concern.

IT WAS TIME to get a job. I hadn't worked in an office for more than five years. I had left my last position—a very fancy, vice presidential job complete with a six-figure salary—to become a writer. I'd published a book that had urged women to broaden their identities and definition of success beyond the traditional male one measured in dollars and business card titles. "Be careful what you write," I thought to myself. "Now you have to live it."

I consciously set out to find a job with less responsibility—one that would allow me more time with my son. It was the height of the venture capital–fueled Wild High-Tech West, and everyone around me was furiously chasing paper riches. The culture of cyber-prospecting had people toiling around the clock, ticking off their net worth in increments of tens of thousands of dollars. I felt like the hot dog vendor at the station, standing idly by as all those high-speed trains whizzed past me.

Within a couple of months, one old-fashioned possibility turned up that fit the bill. It was an editorial job with minimal travel and, best of all, a potentially flexible schedule. Sticking to my new resolve, I asked if I'd be able to work at home three afternoons a week. I was willing to take less salary in exchange. The person doing the hiring didn't love the idea but agreed to give this untraditional arrangement a try.

I had taken a position that paid exactly a quarter of my last salary. In exchange, I could leave at 3:00 P.M. three days a week to pick up my son from school. I could pay my bills and still be around for my son, who had his hands full adjusting to a new school, a new city, and a divorce. "A win-win," I thought.

But this kind of move down the corporate ladder turned out to be a lot harder than it looked. My voluntary step backward was tough for people to understand and harder for me to live with than I had expected. Why didn't I want a bigger job? they wondered. A few people eyed me with suspicion. Was I simply lying in wait like a tiny land mine that would explode on contact and take their jobs away? My own mood swung back and forth between relief at being employed at all and irritation that I had intentionally under-employed myself. During the first few months, my ego would rise up and I would fight (not always with the greatest success) the temptation to parade around my previous positions in order to compensate for my newly diminished stature. Then I would remind my wounded sense of pride that under the circumstances, time was more important than money.

Within a few months, I settled in to my new routine. "This isn't so bad," I thought. I stopped feeling the need to remind myself and others who I used to be and began to really appreciate the flexibility that my new job provided. But then there was a management shake-up, and I was asked to step into a more managerial position, one that would have fed both my wallet and my ego. I felt flattered and grateful. The old me would have snapped it up in a minute. I could start a college fund, replace my stove (not with a six-burner but certainly with one that had more than two functional flames), buy some new clothes and some child care.

I flew to New York uncertain about what I would do. But as I sat in the elegant offices of the woman who would be my new boss—a woman for whom I had profound respect—I found myself telling her that I couldn't take the job. I don't know who was more surprised. "But you can do both," she said. "I raised my kids and had a wonderful career." I knew she was right. It was possible. I had done it myself before. But it wasn't right for me now. Not when I felt my whole life had been turned inside out. I had just gotten my feet back on the ground, and I didn't want to look down and see them scaling the job ladder simply because that's what they were automatically trained to do.

I left her offices completely convinced I had committed career suicide. I understood as well as anyone else the consequences of the decision to place my family life ahead of my work life. As I walked to meet a friend for dinner, I thought about a man I had once interviewed. Edward had been a regional editor for a major national newspaper. Working outside of the home office, he had built a lovely life for himself. Although his first marriage had failed (in part because of his workaholism), in his new marriage he vigilantly guarded the time he spent with his wife and young daughter. Ed had come from a very successful family, and he knew his father expected him to follow his lead; indeed, he measured himself by his father's accomplishments. "In my family, you had to work and had to succeed, and you had to be, if not rich, at least famous," he'd once told me.

Ed had been raised in an environment in which a man's bank balance and business card determined much of his value as a person. He knew he wasn't immune to such pressures. But he'd also watched his father work to the exclusion of his family. He'd seen his mother left alone to raise her children. He didn't want a marriage or a life like his parents'. He knew how important it was for both him and his wife to be gainfully employed, but he struggled with all the traditional roles and expectations.

Ed saw what was in store for him. Because he was a rising star, it was just a matter of time before he was offered another position at the paper—one that would mean that he would no longer have the hours to spend at home raising his daughter. "Maybe it's not possible to be king of the hill and a good father," he told me. "So maybe you wind up making a choice. You make it two-thirds the way up the hill and wind up being perfectly happy there."

For many years, I thought about Ed. His intentions had actually inspired me to propose the work arrangement I now guarded at considerable expense. I hoped to find that I could go partway up the hill and be happy. Arrive at that resting place called "enough."

I mentioned Ed's story over dinner with a friend on the evening I turned down the promotion. It turned out she'd gone to high school with him. "A sign," I thought, giving the universe the big wink I usually reserve for when I find a great parking spot.

"Whatever happened to him?" I asked.

"Oh, you didn't hear?" she said. "He's now a big muckety-muck. Editor in chief. Our kids go to school together, but I don't see him much. I think he travels constantly. He's got two girls. I think the older one has to be almost thirteen by now. He's a huge success."

"And his wife?" I asked.

"Gave up practicing law. We're on the library committee together."

I was crestfallen, but I understood. He had been offered an amazing opportunity, one that would take him to the very top of the hill. But it saddened me because I knew he understood exactly what he'd traded for his success.

WHEN TIME BECOMES more valuable than money, success, or ego, we make different decisions. Not always out of virtue but certainly out of necessity. I'd turned down the promotion but instead proposed a smart, highly qualified candidate for the position. This guy deserved the promotion, and he really wanted it. But looking back, I see now that I'd set a timer on my job that day. My dedication was now suspect. My new boss certainly didn't understand why I'd made the decision I did. He couldn't accept the fact that I honestly did want my flexible schedule more than a VP title on a business card, and he treated me with suspicion, then distrust, and ultimately with such scrutiny that the job became untenable. After a year of trying to resolve our embattled relationship, I left.

I'd walked away from a good job once before. This time it was just as sleep disrupting, but for very different reasons. Now my worries centered on how to support my family, not on questions of identity as they had in the past. I felt plenty scared but also relieved. I still needed money—actually, I needed it more than ever. But I didn't need it the same way. Some of the freight that money carried had been off-loaded.

One by one, the rescue fantasies had disappeared. First Prince Solvency, next the safety of a corporate position. But they were replaced by something else, something surprising—a growing sense of value and security that didn't depend on cash. I felt a nascent sense of worth that had nothing to do with who I was married to or where I worked or what I did every day. Juliet Schor understands my transformation. "In order to transcend that mesmerizing power of money, in order to create lives that are meaningful and authentic and ethical and healthy," she tells me, "you have to get out of that neurotic relationship with money and success and those traditional, conventional values."

Twenty-five years earlier, I had set my sights on

independence, money, success, and a good marriage. They were the north, the south, the east, and the west of my life's compass. I navigated by them each in turn. I had the good fortune to experience a bit of all of them. But what surprises me, as I look back now, is how little thought I gave to valuing the other treasures—like meaning and authenticity. Maybe they required maturity to be appreciated, or perhaps they were simply waiting just beyond youth's horizon.

· 9 ·

MONEY CAN'T BUY ME LOVE

ONE FOGGY, TYPICALLY FREEZING SAN FRANCISCO SUMMER night, I clicked on to Matchmaker.com to check out men. My friend Carole had met the love of her life through this singles Web site, as had another friend, Candice. These women were no urban legends but rather flesh-and-blood people I knew well—fabulous females on the other side of fifty who had logged on and found their soul mates.

"I'm not going on the Internet," I protested the first time Carole suggested it. "I'm not *that* desperate!"

"Try it first," she commanded. "Then tell me you don't like it."

It started with the inevitable questionnaire. How tall, how thin? What my idea of a great date was, where I wanted to be when "the Big One" hit (clearly a San Francisco adaptation), what my zip code was, and how many miles I was willing to travel from it to meet Prince Charming—oh yes, him again. What kind of car did I drive (now we were getting to the subtext), and yes, how much money did I make. Here, there were a range of incomes including two snide alternatives: "What, me work?" and "None of your business."

I filled out the questionnaire as honestly as I could—after all, it was anonymous—lying only about my height (I'm really five-foot-two) because I'd read an article that said that if you were under five-foot-six, you got cut out of a lot of men's searches, and, of course, my weight (I shaved five pounds off; okay, ten), and proceeded to flip through picture after picture of eligible men. Cute, hideous, no way, okay, okay, hmm. I passed over one after another as something disqualified each man.

Then I clicked on someone who looked like Dustin Hoffman's baby brother. Reading down through his profile, I thought, "Cute. Funny. Very funny. Smart. Hmmm." Ooops—there it was: "None of your business." The red fiscal flag went up. Honestly, what man who makes a lot of money isn't all too happy to share it with the world, especially the female half? He also admitted to being under five-foot-six. Next. With a sigh, I turned off the computer.

The following evening, I signed on again, only to find a note waiting in my in-box from Dustin's double. "I feel like I'm writing to myself," the missive started out. The writer proceeded to tick off the answers he'd found in my questionnaire that showed how much we had in common (luckily, honesty wasn't among them). He made me laugh; he was by turns sardonic, thoughtful, warm, and sly. We began to write back and forth furiously, with the hormones and candor that best flourish in the safe shelter of anonymity.

I eyed that "None of your business" line again, weighing how his obvious lack of income might factor into the whole attractiveness quotient. In spite of myself, the flip of a credit card still qualified a gent as a "manly man" in my book, which told me that maybe I hadn't entirely kicked that old "take care of me" thing. But as a middle-aged woman sticking a bunioned foot back into the dating waters, I knew I couldn't be too choosy.

Since my divorce, I'd gone out with two very nice men. One earned a salary so meager that had it been a lightbulb, it would have been impossible to read by. This made it hard for us to do anything more than go to the occasional movie or eat at a very cheap restaurant. The second fellow was quite nice and adorable, but he weighed close to three hundred pounds and consequently had such bad sleep apnea that it was like cuddling up next to a genetic hybrid of Darth Vader and Ling-Ling the panda.

The truth was, I had very little confidence in my own judgment. Hadn't I gone for all the traits I thought were right—manliness, financial soundness, and maturity—when I married my first husband?

Still unsure about how much "None of your business" mattered to me, I agreed to meet Mr. Matchmaker on the following Sunday morning at a café near my house. I decided that he would have to have some pretty hot stuff to get me past my fear that we'd be splitting a four-dollar coffee tab.

. . .

DATING CERTAINLY HAD changed since my twenties and thirties. Now that I was in my midforties and more concerned with how I was going to finish my life than start it, I honestly didn't know what I was supposed to be looking for in a man. The old scripts didn't apply. I didn't need someone to father my children—I was too old to have any more. A provider? Not necessary. I could take care of myself financially. Someone to put a roof over my head? I owned my own home and didn't plan on leaving it. So what is it that we look for when that old checklist no longer applies? Sex? Sure. Love? Of course. But where did my grandmother's admonition about it being just as easy to love a rich man as a poor one come in?

As I wandered farther from the "starter" questions of who I would be, whom I would marry, and how I would earn a living, my values had shifted, dragging my money concerns in their wake. In work, life balance trumped bank balance. My money needs themselves were clearly defined. I knew what I needed to cover home costs, school costs, health care, and to put money aside for my son's college education and my retirement. In my forties, I no longer wondered who I was going to be, just how I was going to pay for who I'd already become.

I also didn't care as much about my appearance, and the amount of money I spent on how I looked (hair coloring aside) occupied a much smaller percentage of my expenditures.

As for my acquisitive nature, having literally moved around the world, I knew only too well that my possessions were becoming more trouble than they were worth. At my fortieth birthday party, I'd covered my dining room table with unopened and unused trinkets, old, dubious wedding presents, and a stunning assortment of candles and candlesticks and asked each guest to please take something away.

Money's value had changed. It had lost its top billing as the central agent of safety and well-being. I had an inner sense of security if not an outer one. It had become a means to an end instead of a goal.

Jean Chatzky says she sees women like me all the time in the course of her writing and research. "I see a difference in older women and younger women," she maintains. "A fifty-year-old absolutely sees money as a means to an end. And a twenty-five-year-old hasn't gotten there yet. Older women have a deeper understanding of what money can and can't do for them. Younger women tend to believe that money has the ability—if not to buy their happiness—then at least to buy the things that make them happy. Older women know that's not true."

Chatzky is right. Money didn't buy me love or happiness in my first marriage. So was I supposed to discount it entirely in my next go-round? In fact, since I had learned that money buys power, I now wondered how my established economic needs and condition would affect a relationship were I to fall in love again and remarry. Would my spouse resent my self-containment? Would I feel free to marry purely for love? Or would I still feel the pull of a potential provider?

"I married my first husband because I thought he was so driven and I was sure he'd take care of us financially," Sandy, a real estate broker in her midforties, tells me as we talk about the important differences between husbands number one and two. "Even though I worked throughout most of our marriage, he made more than I did so the money never felt like mine. That's why I've never been able to blend finances with my current husband. I don't want to do it. If he left, I want to be fine."

While her current husband's financial stability definitely made him appealing to Sandy, she says she married him for his maturity, not for his ability to support her. In fact, she's adamant about keeping her finances separate, and not only because they each have children from previous marriages to care for. "There's a total difference from round one," she says. "But we still argue about money. Ironically, the thing we fight most about is the fact that he won't spend any of it. We have very different philosophies. I believe there's no point in keeping it until after I'm dead. In my angry moments, I tell him he lives in fear about not having enough. He still drives his 'ninety-one Honda with two hundred and fifty thousand miles on it. If he buys a suit, it's from a low budget store like Mervyns. He makes good money. I tell him he can buy a decent suit, but he's too afraid that we'll be forced to leave the house or that we won't have enough for an emergency."

Because Sandy knows she was able to survive on a drastically reduced income after her divorce, she never goes into a panic over money. "I've lived through enough to know that money will come in. And if we lose the house, then we do. I'm a lot more open to life, and if for some reason we had to move, then we had to move."

Sandy's confidence was hard-won. "In my first marriage," she recalls, "I was afraid all the time." But when it ended, she had no choice—she had to support her family. "Who knew that what I learned by going through really tough economic times would be so important to me being who I am now, so important to what I do, so important to my ability to affect the world and other people? I swear I have a great marriage now because of that. I know the traps of looking to someone else to fill the holes in me."

I WASN'T SO sure. On paper I definitely wanted to believe that economic concerns weren't going to dictate romantic ones, but I'd yet to test-drive these new convictions. Unsure of my own potential reaction, I entered that coffee shop where I was to meet Mr. Matchmaker.

While I'm not sure that I believe in love at first sight, I can now make a pretty good argument for it by the third date. Steve (I couldn't believe he had the same name as my ex-husband) says he knew within moments after we met that we'd be married. I'm not sure I did. All I know is I felt as if I'd found something precious that I'd misplaced years earlier. Something as familiar to me as my own skin. "There you are," I thought, and just like that, money was the last thing on my mind.

But not for long. Those first few weeks of falling in love may suspend all differences, but sooner or later, gravity exerts itself and we come back down to earth. One month into our courtship, we had our moment of financial reckoning. I had gone to New York for a business trip, and we used the distance between us to exchange e-mails on the one topic that we both feared could stop our new love in its tracks: money. By then I was head over heels, but this correspondence got my complete attention.

"During my married years," he wrote, "my ex-wife and I were on our way toward at least a comfortable lifestyle— including, of course, the benefits and leverage that accrue from home ownership in the most expensive housing market in the country. Things changed dramatically for me in the first couple of years after the separation and divorce. For a while I worked only part-time and supplemented my lowered income by running up a couple of credit cards to their limits and (stupidly, oh-so-stupidly) withdrawing money from my IRA. My accountant at the time said I would've been better off robbing a bank and taking my chances of not getting caught. Eventually, I regained relative equilibrium by returning to full-time work. But some of the damage has remained unresolved."

I began to sweat cold beads of panic as he went on to detail his salary and his status with his creditors. This was not the picture of a man I could marry. Or was it? I reminded myself that I didn't need his financial protection, and that other things might matter more.

I read on. "Normally, I would feel so incredibly awkward—if not completely resistant—in baring my financial soul (oh, what an improper oxymoron that is), but I do it without any sense of embarrassment (well, not too much anyway) because I don't want there to be any large, mysterious gaps between us. God," he ended, "I've rambled— undoubtedly a sign of some nervous energy and lingering anxiety/apprehension about delving into such ticklish matters. No doubt that's also because I'm acutely aware of, shall we say, seeming disparities in our respective fiscal report cards."

"Well," I thought. "You have to admire the man's candor." And sitting there in front of the computer I felt a flush of shame at my shallowness. I knew how I wanted to respond—that his money history didn't matter. But it still sort of did. I put my fingers to the keyboard, now firmly in unfamiliar territory.

"Unlike you," I began, "I have been very fortunate on the financial front—even before my marriage, money was something I knew how to make. I think because I felt emotionally and familialy (is that a word?) insecure, I figured out that the way to real freedom and safety was through my earning power. It became a priority for me." ("True," I said to myself as I wrote, "even if I did manage to lose sight of it.")

I continued typing: "Maybe I am naive here, but as long as we work this through in the moment things arise—and they will—and you are taking care of what you need to take care of, I just don't care what you do or don't make."

I paused, wondering if that last sentence was truly honest or simply wishful thinking. Deciding it was a little of both, I pushed forward. "But this money imbalance cuts both ways. Are you going to resent that I have a decent amount of money in my retirement account, that I make a good salary and have child support?" I divulged the fine print because I wanted him to know my exact financial status because, as I told him, our different fiscal profiles had the potential to erode our relationship. I mentioned how I'd lost respect for the first man I had dated because he was unwilling to go out and make an adult living, which I saw as the petulant entitlement of a man who didn't want to take responsibility for himself and who hid behind his identity as "an artist."

Continuing, I stumbled on the truth. "It is, in the end, the responsibility factor that engenders the respect. Still, in all candor, I like the feeling of being taken care of. And I think in the past, I have equated that with money. So I can promise you this: I won't let things fester. If something is bothering me, I will not ambush you with it or let it come out sideways but talk to you. I want and need an equal partner. Money has an insidious power to disrupt equality. We have an imbalance. Let's figure out how to deal with it.

"All this only matters because we are developing a relationship of equals. I need to respect you as much as you need to respect me. This is as honest as I can possibly be on this difficult subject, but I suppose nothing is more intimate in a funny way than the money stuff, but that is the tough intimacy."

I may have lied through my teeth about my weight, but I had come clean about money, risking all, because I had discovered that respect mattered more to me than the fantasy of financial dependency. We may not have known what was going to happen, but we knew our starting points and what each of us needed in order to respect the other.

THE SEVERING OF love and money is extremely important for women and not just because it opens us up to more fully rounded attachments. The magical thinking that often accompanies fantasies of financial dependency can and does ultimately impoverish women. Men don't confuse the two. And we shouldn't either.

When we separate love and money, it forces us to focus on both, but as separate entities. Why is this important? Because nine out of ten women will be financially on their own at some point in their lives. More than half of American women have no pension coverage (versus only a quarter of men), and one in four women are broke within two months of their husbands' deaths. On average, women live seven years longer than their husbands, and over three-quarters of all women are widowed at an average age of fifty-six.[1] Women comprise a horrifying 87 percent of the impoverished elderly.[2]

There comes a point in all women's lives where we have to take command of our economic destinies. Some women do it early on. I started saving for my retirement in my twenties, more out of a combination of neurosis and the fact that my company offered a savings plan than for any strategic or virtuous reason. But many women wait until a major life change takes place: We marry (or don't) and want a house and realize we can't afford one. We lose a job, a husband loses a job, we lose husbands, we fall ill or someone else does, or death strikes. At each of these points, money comes into play and causes us to evaluate our assets with a critical eye.

When we detach emotions and money, we can take the steps we need to in order to avoid feeling helpless. According to a survey from the National Center for Women and Retirement, of those women who say they feel in control of their lives, 56 percent of them saved and invested monthly. Of the 42 percent who said they felt out of control, only 17 percent made saving and investing for retirement a priority. There's a direct correlation between how well a woman takes care of herself financially and how good she feels about herself.[3]

So why don't more women take care of themselves? This is the question that has spawned a mini-industry of "Smart Women Finish Rich" books. It's right up there with "Why can't I lose the last ten pounds?" The answers are clear: If you want to lose weight, exercise more and eat less. If you want financial control, save more and spend less. Take time to learn about investing.

But all those truths still haven't spawned a contagion of fiscal responsibility. We may know what to do, but we lack the means, the discipline, or the confidence to do it. "No one in her right mind wants to make a mistake with her money," says the financial expert Barbara Stanny. "We're not dealing just with dollars but with our sense of security."

That's the point, though, isn't it? We don't want to play games with our sense of security. We may have buried our heads in wishful thinking and procrastinated about financial health, but eventually something happens to each one of us that forces us to take responsibility. When we do, two fears repeatedly crop up: the fear of making a mistake and failing, and the fear of the unknown. The 2001 Women's Cents Study, which surveyed thousands of women between the ages of twenty-one and seventy-five, reported that "while women are increasingly adopting healthy attitudes about money, psychological traits prevent them from acting on those beliefs." More than 54 percent of the women surveyed had postponed making a financial decision for fear of making a mistake, while 58 percent said they just didn't know or understand how to make and manage their investments.[4]

Like many women, I identified with those anxieties. In 1999, I devoted at least fourteen seconds to financial research when it came time to invest my retirement funds. I called my friend Carole. "I'm up twenty-five percent in the market," she said. "Sounds good enough for me," I responded and moved all my money to her investment broker. "I'm a single mother," I told the nice lady. "Please invest this as you would if you were one, too. This is all I have." For a few months, I was a financial genius. The value of my money soared. I could do no wrong. I was set for life. I started planning my retirement.

What a chump.

Within the year, the stock market tanked, taking my balance with it. With my capital sliced in half, I panicked, pulled everything away from the nice broker, sold all my high-tech stocks (creating a huge tax problem), and immediately overcorrected by placing whatever was left in the closest investment equivalent to hiding it under a mattress that I could find. I let my emotions call the shots and consequently made every mistake possible.

Uncomfortably aware that my ignorance caused my ineptitude, I went out and bought a dozen investment books. Each offered more or less the same information. Make a budget, save a portion of everything you make. Assess your risk tolerance (what risk tolerance?). Educate yourself. Take control. Overcome your inner psychological demons that keep you too afraid or anxious to do all of the above.

I guess that's where I got stuck.

Yes, some of the wisdom in these books did sink in. I realized there was no mystery to investing, aside from the location of the little battery inside me that powered a seemingly inexhaustible supply of fear. But none of the books helped me sleep one bit better at night. Instead, their admonitions actually became a new checklist for all the ways in which I was not taking proper care of my future.

Resigned to my responsibilities, I have slowly chipped away at my nervous condition by adhering to the fiscal equivalent of Weight Watchers. No magical intervention was going to set things right. Instead I was going to have to settle for small increments of economic progress, such as setting aside modest amounts of savings every month for my IRA. I found a new job because I had to make more money. I did not replace the cracking walls and cracked, dingy sink counter in my son's bathroom because, given the choice between my own dotage and some aging and unappealing tiles, I decided to put the cash where I knew it belonged. The bathroom may not be a thing of beauty, but the restful sleep that resulted from knowing I was doing right by my family sure was.

With every tiny, responsible action, my emotional resistance to taking care of myself financially began to fall away. There was no secret code involved in budgeting and investing—at least not one that some attention and discipline couldn't crack. As for the subtler, more evasive riddle of who was going to make sure I would be okay in my old age, that question fell in the face of the very liberating—but relentlessly realistic—acceptance that that person was me.

This sounds like it was a revelation. It wasn't. The perverse thing is, I had been a financially independent and fiscally responsible woman for many years. But even though I had the skills, I still lacked the confidence. I was like the women that the psychologist Stephen Goldbart had observed over and over again in his practice. Women who are extremely capable, and who don't hesitate to manage their businesses' budgets, but who become disaster cases when it comes to managing their own financial lives. This lack of confidence is a strange, female phenomenon with no simple origin. Experts may offer varieties of explanations ranging from the rapid revolution in gender-based financial expectations, to overly supportive parents, to the ease with which we can get ourselves into massive credit card debt, but one thing is clear: for whatever combination of reasons, many women find themselves in the paradoxical economic state where they can earn money but not hold on to it. As women approach middle age, they start to feel the repercussions of this problem. Elise becomes agitated the minute we start talking about how *sick* it is (her word) that she spent most of her career as a bank loan officer, handling huge corporate loans, but is unable to pay down her MasterCard bill. At fifty-one, she's never been married and she's never saved very much. What she does have, she spends on her home. She's knows she has a finite amount of time left to prepare for her future, but she's locked into such high housing expenses that she has very little money left at the end of each month to put into savings.

Elise resembles one of the fifty thousand men and women profiled by the financial psychologist Kathleen Gurney. Gurney found that women evidenced more emotion and less confidence around money than men did, and that a large segment of women earned high incomes but had very little to show for it. She concluded that women used spending therapeutically. "Instead of dealing with their emotions, they were acting them out." [5]

Elise has been taking antidepressants for two years, ever since she experienced setbacks in her job and her health. "I had been making a good living and had a nice career. But then two years ago, I was passed over for a promotion. Then I got this autoimmune disease and got really sick. I had to go on disability and was refused medical coverage due to a prior condition. I took a second mortgage on my apartment to pay for medical expenses. I didn't have much savings— I'd spent most of it fixing up my home. I borrowed from my parents. I still couldn't work. I've held on to my house, but just barely, and I've borrowed so heavily against it, I no longer have much equity left. Honestly, I don't know what I'm going to do. I guess I'll figure it out when I get there."

Decades of financial irresponsibility caught up with Elise. When we don't look our finances squarely in the eye, when we hide behind our sense of entitlement, our wishful thinking, or immediate gratifications, we ultimately end up like Elise—high on a hill overlooking an indistinct and underfunded future.

AS FOR ME, the one-two punch of losing much of my nest egg in the stock crash and the prospect of sharing what was left with a man who had saved next to nothing for his own retirement brought out some complex emotions, to say the least. After we dated for about a year, Steve No. 2 (as my friends called him) and his daughter moved into the little house on the hill where my son and I lived with our cat and dog. We were engaged to be married. We'd just taken out a home equity loan (which, I noted to myself, was on *my* line of credit) in order to renovate the house so that it had more than one full bathroom. (The need for a second bathroom was underscored one morning when I looked out the window and saw my then six-year-old son peeing in the backyard bushes. "What are you doing?" I shrieked. "The bathroom was tooken," he said. "And I had to go real bad.")

Taking my newfound financially responsible attitude to heart, I asked Steve to sign a prenuptial agreement, which he happily did. We decided to pool our finances. (It turns out that he makes a respectable living as a journalist.) Even if I was bringing a bit more to the table, it made more sense to put everything together. For a while, this worked without a hitch.

Then one afternoon, the phone rang. "My car died," said my brand-new husband. Dead cars on San Francisco hills are bad things. A week later, he headed off to the car dealer. We had agreed that as long as we had the home equity line of credit, we might as well use it to pay for a new car rather than finance it. To me, this was a theoretical discussion, much like the one we'd had about the prenuptial. A just-in-case scenario. Not so to him. A few hours later, he drove up to the house in a secondhand, $17,000 blue Volkswagen convertible.

"I thought you said you were just going to *look* at cars," I squeaked, my voice a full octave higher than normal.

"Well, this was a really good deal, so I took it," he answered, not realizing until then that this might have been better handled as a joint decision. As Deborah Tannen points out in *You Just Don't Understand,* women and men really do communicate differently when it comes to purchases. I had wanted to be included; he thought we'd already had the discussion. One look at my shocked expression told him that we had some work to do on our communication skills and the management of our finances. To me, it sure felt like this was *my* money he was spending, *my* retirement, *my* debt, even though we both contributed to the pot and were jointly responsible.

I had leapfrogged from financial independence directly into financial control freak. Just like the women in a recent Japanese survey, I tended to be more careful about my money than men. "Tightfisted," said the headline in the *Mainichi Daily News.*[6] That definitely seemed to apply here.

I wondered if this is how men feel when their wives earn less yet spend more. "Oh, I joke about it," Alan, Kelly's stockbroker husband, confides to me. "I once calculated that if she ever died, even after paying for a sitter for the kids and whatnot, I'd be saving money. When I tell her this, she gets so pissed off, but I hope she knows I'm only kidding. Actually, it makes me happy to be able to do it." To Alan, watching his wife spend lots of money is a sign that he's made it. He's proud that he's got the money for her to spend. But where Alan felt a flush of pride, I felt a stab of irritation bordering on downright anger toward my husband.

I treated my husband's next big purchase—a computer with more memory than an entire class of geniuses—as a fiscal alert, a survival alarm bell, an attack on our long-range security, a loss of control. And following on the heels of my anger? Guilt at feeling pissed off. Here was this magnificent guy, and all I could think about was that he was spending and threatening our retirement and security. Like I didn't spend a fortune on things for the house or the garden. I felt like a heel.

"That's because your brain is literally different than his," Louann Brizendine reminds me when I describe my conflict. "The reason you feel guilt is because you're doing something to fulfill a basic, primitive need—making sure there's enough money for your family. But you have a higher self in mind. The guilt is the difference between fulfilling that fundamental need—in this case having enough money for a cushion—and dealing with some kind of higher ideal of your self-image."

Brizendine knows the conflict well. "I even feel conflicted about saying this because I chose to become a doctor in part because I wanted to be financially self-sustaining. I remember telling one of the women physicians who interviewed me for medical school that I didn't want anyone to be able to tell me what to do. I wanted freedom. I went for the goal of having a profession and the goal of supporting myself. I came from a poor family, and being financially independent was to me the greatest good. I knew zero dollars were coming from my family. I left home at seventeen and never saw a penny."

But there's no discounting the influence of women's brain chemistry no matter what our intentions are, Brizendine points out. "When I was in medical school, my boyfriend and I had decided that everything was going to be fifty-fifty when we married. We were each going to work half-time, parent half-time, contribute half-time. But you don't realize your brain is literally going to change when you have kids. All those hormones rearrange it. Women have additional obstacles to going to work in a workplace designed for men," Brizendine continues. "And for a while we can act just as they do in it. But when a woman has a child, it's not a life-changing experience; it's a brain-changing experience. We are biologically wired to make sure there's enough money to take care of our kids. Anything that threatens that is going to evoke a pretty primitive reaction."

I GREW TO love my husband's impulsively purchased car (although to him this was no impulse—just a needed expenditure), especially on the three or four days a year when it's warm and sunny enough in San Francisco to put the top down. And despite my enormous love for him I still occasionally wince when some new computer gadget shows up at our doorstep.

But sitting at the kitchen table one evening some four years into our marriage, in the middle of the usual discussions about homework and boyfriends and the logistics of the weekend's sporting events, I realized that the biggest promise money ever made to me had come true. And it turned out that it had nothing to do with love or dependency or social status or even need. It was simply this: If I carved out a place in my life to take care of my finances in the same way and with the same lack of emotional charge that I paid my electric bill, bought my groceries, and got my car tuned up, then money would help support the people I loved. Nothing more and nothing less.

EPILOGUE: MARK TWAIN WAS RIGHT
(OR WAS IT THOMAS JEFFERSON?)

IT'S YET ANOTHER FOGGY AND UNDERCAFFEINATED Saturday morning in May. My son is on the baseball team of the Blithe and Untalented—the more competitive and athletically ambitious types having departed his Park and Recreation League for the more accomplished and aggressive Little League teams. The somewhat self-selecting parents—no bankers or venture capitalists here but instead a couple of writers, a seamstress, a nurse, a bartender, and an environmental attorney—have huddled together in the bleachers rooting for our hapless kids who've just had to rope in a large kindergartner and the wiry nephew of one of the coaches to fill up the roster for the 10:00 A.M. game.

I am talking to one of the writers, a guy who's really good at what he does—as well as rich and famous. He's also rather nicer than I thought he'd be, although I have my antennae raised and quivering, poised to pick up incoming slights. I'm ready to defend myself against the first sign of superiority. But for this inning, I've become an intimate, or at least enough of a known quantity, that his guard drops, and we start to talk, our freezing hands clasped tightly around cooling coffees.

We're talking about his fame. How he really enjoys it. How he likes being recognized, complimented by strangers. I appreciate his candor. Too many people want what he has with all their hearts, only to stuff all that hunger into falsely modest dress. No, this fellow feels he's worked hard, and he really appreciates his success. He freely admits that he likes being rich and not worrying about money.

This Saturday morning, the usual envy tinged with insufficiency that such conversations can elicit in me is oddly absent. Instead, I find myself seriously considering what Famous Writer is saying. Don't get me wrong. Would I like to have a piece of his action? Certainly. But my self-worth doesn't plummet in the face of his achievement. I feel no meagerness in the face of his abundance. Instead, I become aware of a new feeling. It must have been creeping up on me for some time but has now reached the point where it occupies more of my consciousness than less.

I realize that I'm very satisfied with my current circumstances. Maybe I have fewer choices than I did ten years ago, but something about these limited options makes me appreciate all the more what I do have. Life feels manageable. For the moment, I've tasted "enough."

Some of the changes that have brought me to this point

have been intentional; others took place simply as fallout from events beyond my control. All I know, as I clasp my coffee, is that I've stumbled into a new place, one where, amazingly, I have more inner security than outer security—and that's just fine with me.

The fiscal facts don't immediately support this new equilibrium. My income is exactly half of what it was a decade ago. We have a minimal college fund started for our son, but we have nothing saved for our daughter as we started too late to do her any good. My retirement balance has still not recovered from the nosedive it took five years earlier. We own our home, and we have a mortgage that doesn't break the bank. Our credit card debts usually fall below the national average. But if my husband or I were to lose our job, or if one of us were to come down with a debilitating illness, we'd be in deep trouble. All that aside, on this morning, we are healthy, and I realize that more often than not, I've been sleeping peacefully through the night. Between my husband's income and mine, we have enough money to live and cope with relatively normal, everyday anxieties.

Like my son, I've stepped out of the competitive leagues even if I'm still in the game swinging. "I don't care if I'm not on the 'A' team," he told me not long ago, with the wisdom of someone uncontaminated by experience. "I just want to play and have fun." Sitting on these bleachers, I see that through no virtue of my own, I too have stopped trying to make it to the luxury leagues. My goal is simply to enjoy my life, along with a little security. Maybe it's my version of

Thomas Jefferson's dream for Americans—the one that begins with "life, liberty, and the pursuit of happiness."

A change in my material desires has contributed greatly to my new sense of calm. Yes, I still think it would be lovely to have a double oven. Yes, I continue to thumb through home design magazines while under the hairdresser's ministration, salivating over Sub-Zero refrigerators that look like china cabinets. But I am no longer willing to place having beautiful possessions—and the time and money it takes to get them—high up on my to-do list. I see all too clearly the price I have paid to secure what I have always thought of as the dream life. I am not willing to go into emotional debt any longer.

The advertisers may have initially commanded my complete attention with their promises of perfection by acquisition and association, but eventually I faced the true cost of buying into these fantasies. I learned that if I want to have everyone at the dinner table, I have to be there too, which, for me, means trading salary for supper. I've taken the risky path of downscaling my work and salary in exchange for less stress and fewer hours, and the experience has revealed that scaling back had an unexpected side effect: Once I started putting my life before my dreams, my appetite for the trophies of traditional success diminished. Like a dieter whose stomach has shrunk, I feel more satisfied more quickly with less. If I compare myself to others, I try to restrict my comparison to where I've come from, and not to what others have or where I want to be. As a result, I am finding more pleasure in what I actually possess.

David Myers's research on what creates happiness backs up my experience. He found that when we feel we should live a certain way, or should have as much as our neighbors, friends, and colleagues, it's very hard to reach a point of satisfaction. "Just as comparing ourselves with those who are better off creates envy, counting our blessings as we compare ourselves with those less well off boosts our contentment," says Myers.[1] "Seeking happiness through material achievement requires an ever-increasing abundance of things." We constantly need more—more money, more things—to maintain a level of euphoria. "Wealth is like health," he concludes. "Its utter absence breeds misery, but having it doesn't guarantee happiness."

This isn't headline news. But there's a huge difference between knowing this intellectually and grappling our way to this simple understanding. I'm like those people that motivational speaker Zig Ziglar talks about when he says: "Money won't make you happy. But everyone wants to find that out for themselves." I had to find my own way—a way that meant separating my emotions from my cash.

MY EXPERIENCE IS not unique. I've learned that as women age, our attitudes and values about money shift. While no statistical measurements exist, it's worth observing that as an unprecedented number of women move toward the end of our child-bearing or child-raising years, there does seem to be a reevaluation of the bargains we made with cash to ensure our financial security. Money's mystery departs and takes with it much of the emotional hungers we've looked to money to satisfy. Some of this results from age and experience, from which none of us are immune. We've learned that being "good girls" doesn't ultimately pay. Disappointments, reversals, divorce, or death have taught us that we have to take direct responsibility for our financial lives. As we become released by time from the more traditional roles of wife, mother, nurturer, we become less distinguishable from men who are simultaneously passing the zeniths of their "provider" demands. (I'm not sure why this point in a man's life is typically called a midlife "crisis." As I see it, anything that offers a man a way of according more value to time than money is a revelation.)

In a poll conducted in 2004 by the Center for the New American Dream, nearly half of those interviewed reported that they had made voluntary changes in their lives that resulted in more time and less money, and were happy that they did. A majority felt our society's priorities were "out of whack," with working and making money put ahead of family and community. Finally, those polled were very concerned about our culture's excessive materialism and worried about its impact on our children.[2]

But if we adults may be experiencing a dawning awareness of money's emotional limits, we sure haven't given our kids the same message. In fact, just as we're beginning to see the limits of money, our children are embracing their material sides with full ardor. The University of California at Los Angeles began studying incoming freshmen in 1966—and now has data on more than twenty thousand of them. Beginning in 1978, researchers noticed a change in the students' levels of materialism. Almost all incoming freshmen from that year forward said that being well-off financially was more important to their overall happiness than developing a meaningful life philosophy. Those numbers have held steady for twenty-plus years.[3]

I suppose this finding isn't surprising—not in a world where marketing companies, hoping to create buzz and new trends among so-called tweens (that transitional age group between eight and thirteen), provide twelve-year-old girls at sleepover parties with goodie baskets of products they want the girls to promote. These marketers are all too aware of our children's material appetites and disposable income, which comes, of course, from their parents. Tweens directly spend $10 billion each year and influence another $74 billion's worth of family spending.[4]

Is this what the future holds? In 2003, the average American household's savings fell to a record low—less than two-tenths of one percent of disposable income. That works out to a meager $1.50 a week for a family whose take-home pay averages $40,000 dollars per year.[5] In 2003, the average American household spent 13 percent of its after-tax income to pay debts—largely mortgages and car loans.[6] No wonder someone goes bankrupt in the United States every fifteen seconds.[7]

When we consider that over our lifetime the majority of

women will have earned less than men, these numbers only get worse. Given the reality that half of all women work in jobs without pensions,[8] we can't afford not to take an active role in our financial lives. According to a 2004 report released by the Federal Reserve, only 35 percent of single women had retirement accounts, and only 8 percent had traditional pensions.[9] The combination of a lifetime of financial inequalities and extended life expectancy creates tremendous vulnerabilities for women. With so much at stake for us, we cannot allow our emotions to blind us to our realities.

I don't want this for my friends and I certainly don't want this for my children. But when my husband and I try to impart to them the importance of developing a personal safety net of savings (as opposed to, say, buying a new video game or a new pair of jeans), we might as well be whistling past the fiscal graveyard. Saving their money, we tell them, will buy them peace of mind and many choices in life. Spending it now will provide a few hours of pleasure. We try to drive the point home by telling them it will take them several weeks' worth of allowance to afford purchases whose luster will fade more quickly.

Our children understand that they are advertising targets. But they think they're in control of their desires. While I would like to believe in their self-confidence, I know what they're up against. The science of creating material appetites is far more powerful than they are. We are living in an $11 trillion economy, two-thirds of which is based in consumerism.[10] Is this the legacy we want to pass on to the next generation? When Juliet Schor recently surveyed ten- to thirteen-year-olds, almost two-thirds of them said their goal was to make a lot of money and be rich when they grew up.

Like their parents before them, today's kids are reaching for their taste of luxury, not realizing that those who can truly afford it live in another world. I tell my children that buying a $60,000 luxury car means next to nothing to a celebrity actor or singer who earns millions of dollars each year. Still, in the face of our consumer culture, these messages are drowned out by the noise generated by the desire machines.

Undoubtedly, our children will have to learn about the limits of materialism the way we did, by experience. Still, it's hard for parents to watch as their sons and daughters start to equate emotions like happiness and satisfaction with the act of acquiring. Like my father, I want to express my love for my children through what I can bequeath them after my death. But I also want them to inherit the spiritual riches that I've gained from losing my illusions about what money can and can't do for me.

A month or two before she died, I asked my best friend's eighty-four-year-old mother about her emotional relationship with money. She looked at me strangely, her blue eyes clouded—as if she didn't really understand the question. I wasn't sure if her brain tumor was scrambling things or if the question itself didn't make sense to her.

After a moment, she said, "When I have it, I'm happy."

"Me too," I thought. But there's a difference between that and *equating* money with happiness.

As long as I had believed that financial security purchased emotional security, I'd lived a dependent, conditional life. Conditional on the individuals, families, institutions— even fantasies—that I'd invested with the power to take care of me. When I made that quiet contract with cash so long ago, I'd trusted that money would compensate for my emotional needs. As a result, each time one of those sources of security disappointed me or disappeared, I was left in a state of fear.

I still have those memories of money. But now I realize that rather than mortgage myself for a Viking range dream life on a layaway plan, I prefer the rather nice General Electric kind of life I've stumbled into—one that can reliably cook a very satisfying dinner. I drive a more or less dependable car that has gone from carrying baby seats to football equipment, and from playing Raffi cassettes to rap on the radio. My still-active desire for a double oven has less to do with signaling that I belong to a certain class or have reached a type of perfection and more to do with the fact that I still haven't figured out how to otherwise make a pot roast and an apple pie at the same time. So I make the pie ahead of time and reheat it. Big deal.

But it is a big deal. I think once more about Ed with his forsaken dream of traveling only two-thirds up the hill and being content with his life. And I think of how our culture conspires against that dream.

I think it was Mark Twain who said, "Happiness is wanting what you have, not having what you want." I tell my kids this, hoping they will learn to balance the act of pursuing with the act of savoring. And each time I repeat this old saw, I count the seconds until one of them rolls their eyeballs.

Still, some of it might just sink in somewhere.

You never know.

NOTES

PROLOGUE: MONEY, A MEMOIR

1. Nomura Securities Company study, reported in the *Mainichi Daily News,* February 3, 2005.
2. Elizabeth Warren and Amelia Warren Tyagi, *The Two-Income Trap: Why Middle-Class Parents Are Going Broke* (Basic Books, 2003), p. iv.
3. Ibid., p. 6.

CHAPTER 1: SECRETS AND LIES

1. Olivia Millan and Karina Piskaldo, "Men, Women and Money," *Psychology Today,* January–February 1999.
2. *Redbook–Smart Money* survey, reported by Walecia Konrad in "The Truth About Men, Women and Money," *Redbook Online,* 2004.
3. U.S. Bureau of Labor Statistics, 2004.
4. Analisa Balares, "'Buycott': 85 Broads and WSA Celebrate Women's Buying Power," *Harbus Online,* October 18, 2004.
5. Lois P. Frankel, "Nice Girls Don't Get Rich," from MSNBC Interactive, May 18, 2005.

6. Whirlpool Foundation, *Women, the New Providers,* May 1995.

7. *Yearning for Balance: Views of Americans on Consumption, Materialism, and the Environment* (prepared for the Merck Family Fund), 1995, p. 20.

8. WISER and the National Center on Women and Aging, *Widowhood: Why Women Need to Talk About This Issue* (funded by the U.S. Administration on Aging), 2003.

9. U.S. Bureau of Labor Statistics, *Highlights of Women's Earnings in 2002,* September 2003.

10. Interep, *All About Women: Demographic, Media and Spending Profiles,* March 2003. (Based on fall 2002 findings by MediaMark Research.)

11. This statistic comes from the National Center for Women and Retirement Research (NCWRR), Women's Cents Study, 1995.

12. Ibid.

13. Ibid.

14. Ibid.

15. Ibid.

CHAPTER 2: THE EMOTIONAL MIDDLE CLASS

1. Michael Silverstein, *Business Week Online,* 2004.

2. Jeff Madrick, "Economic Scene," *New York Times,* June 10, 2004.

3. Andrew Becker, "The Battle over Share of Wallet," from the series *The Secret History of the Credit Card, Frontline,* PBS, http://www.pbs.org/wgbh/pages/frontline/shows/credit/more/battle.html.

4. Suze Orman, "The Pursuit of Cold, Hard Happiness," *O, the Oprah Magazine,* March 2004.

5. Janny Scott and David Leonhardt, "Class in America," *New York Times,* May 15, 2005.

6. Steve Lohr, "America Got Debt?" *New York Times,* December 5, 2004.

7. *Redbook* and *Smart Money,* "Happy Couples Survey," ivillage, June 23, 2004.

8. According to the Women's Cents Study underwritten by the Women's Institute for a Secure Retirement, more than 58 percent of female baby boomers have less than $10,000 saved in a pension plan or 401(k) plan.

CHAPTER 3: FAMILY MONEY

1. Victoria Secunda, "Salary Warfare: When You Make More Than Your Husband," http://www.makingbreadmagazine.com/2004.

2. Ann Crittenden, *The Price of Motherhood* (Henry Holt, 2001), p. 5.

3. Ibid., p. 6.

CHAPTER 4: WORKING GIRL

1. U.S. Bureau of Labor Statistics, *Highlights of Women's Earnings in 2002.*

2. Lisa Barron's study is reported in Kimberly Blanton, "What Men Have That Women Don't," *Boston Globe,* December 28, 2003.

3. Quoted in ibid.

4. U.S. Bureau of Labor Statistics, *Highlights of Women's Earnings in 2002.*

CHAPTER 5: YOU CAN NEVER BE TOO RICH OR TOO THIN

1. http://www.Common Sense Media.org/2003/research.

2. Christine Doyle, "Nip and Tuck: We're All Up for It," *London Daily Telegraph* (online edition), January 25, 2005.

3. Michael Olding and Diana Zuckerman cite this statistic in "Cosmetic Surgery and Teens," *Washington Post,* October 26, 2004.

CHAPER 6: FOR RICHER OR POORER

1. Randi Minetor, *Breadwinner Wives and the Men They Marry: How to Have a Successful Marriage While Outearning Your Husband* (New Horizon Press, 2002), p. 6.

2. Rutgers University, *State of the Unions,* http://www.legalhelper.net/ui/news/premarital-agreement-news-3.aspx/2004.

3. Walecia Konrad, "The Truth About Men, Women and Money," *Redbook Online,* 2004.

4. Ibid.

5. Yankelovich Partners, *A Study About Money,* March 13, 2001.

6. This survey is cited in Janet Kidd Stewart, *Chicago Tribune* (online edition), May 8, 2005.

7. Warren and Tyagi, *The Two-Income Trap,* p. 5.

8. "Understanding the Mom Market," http://www.BSMMedia .com, 2001–02.

CHAPTER 7: THE DEATH OF THE INNER STEWARDESS

1. Lenore Weitzman's statistic is cited in Warren and Tyagi, *The Two-Income Trap,* p. 99.

2. Ibid., p. 220.

3. Ibid., p. 9.

4. Ibid., pp. 9, 104.

5. Ibid., p. 9.

6. David G. Myers, "Happiness," online excerpt from *Psychology,* 7th ed. (Worth, 2004).

7. Ibid.

8. Ibid.

9. Quoted in ibid.

10. Barbara Stanny, *Prince Charming Isn't Coming: How Women Get Smart About Money* (Penguin, 1997), p. 21.

11. From the Investment Company Institute study as reported in http://www.Thirdage.com/new/archive/980509-02.html.

CHAPTER 8: EGOCIDE (OR DOWNWARD MOBILITY)

1. Catalyst, "Buying Power," Catalyst Quick Take, updated May 6, 2004.

CHAPTER 9: MONEY CAN'T BUY ME LOVE

1. Based on U.S. Bureau of Labor Statistics, "Women and Money," MsMoney.com, August 24, 2004.

2. Ibid.

3. National Center for Women and Retirement, Women's Cents Study, 2001.

4. Ibid.

5. Stanny, *Prince Charming Isn't Coming,* p. 87.

6. Nomura Securities Company study, reported in the *Mainichi Daily News,* February 3, 2005.

EPILOGUE: MARK TWAIN WAS RIGHT

1. Myers, "Happiness."

2. *New American Dream Survey Report,* September 2005, p. 2.

3. The American Freshman surveys, UCLA, 1966–2002.

4. "The Power of Tweens," *Chicago Tribune,* September 4, 2002.

5. Steve Lohr, "Maybe It's Not All Your Fault," *New York Times,* December 5, 2004.

6. Ibid.

7. Ibid.

8. Women's Institute for Secure Retirement, 2002.

9. Mary Duenwald and Bernard Stamler, "On Their Own, in the Same Boat," *New York Times,* April 13, 2004.

10. Women's Institute for Secure Retirement, 2002.

SELECTED BIBLIOGRAPHY

Babcock, Linda, and Sara Laschever. *Women Don't Ask: Negotiation and the Gender Divide.* Princeton University Press, 2003.

Bach, David. *Smart Women Finish Rich: 9 Steps to Achieving Financial Security and Funding Your Dreams.* Broadway Books, 1999.

Brizendine, Louann, and Susan Wels. *The Female Brain.* Morgan Road Books, 2006.

Crittenden, Ann. *The Price of Motherhood: Why the Most Important Job in the World Is Still the Least Valued.* Henry Holt, 2001.

de Graaf, John, David Wann, and Thomas Naylor. *Affluenza: The All-Consuming Epidemic.* Illustrations by David Horsey. Berrett-Koehler, 2001.

Dominguez, Joe, and Vicki Robin. *Your Money or Your Life: Transforming Your Relationship with Money and Achieving Financial Independence.* Penguin Books, 1992.

Easterbrook, Gregg. *The Progress Paradox: How Life Gets Better While People Feel Worse.* Random House, 2004.

Ehrenreich, Barbara. *Nickel and Dimed: On (Not) Getting By in America.* Henry Holt, 2001.

Godfrey, Joline. *Raising Financially Fit Kids.* Ten Speed Press, 2003.

Klainer, Pamela York. *How Much Is Enough? Harness the Power of Your Money Story—and Change Your Life.* Basic Books, 2002.

Minetor, Randi. *Breadwinner Wives and the Men They Marry: How to Have a Successful Marriage While Outearning Your Husband.* New Horizon Press, 2002.

Orman, Suze. *The Money Book for the Young, Fabulous and Broke.* Riverhead Books, 2005.

———. *Nine Steps to Financial Freedom: Practical and Spiritual Steps So You Can Stop Worrying.* Three Rivers Press, 1997.

Schor, Juliet B. *Born to Buy: The Commercialized Child and the New Consumer Culture.* Scribner, 2004.

———. *The Overspent American: Why We Want What We Don't Need.* Basic Books, 1998.

———. *The Overworked American: The Unexpected Decline of Leisure.* Basic Books, 1992.

Stanny, Barbara. *Prince Charming Isn't Coming: How Women Get Smart About Money.* Penguin Books, 1997.

Tannen, Deborah. *Talking from 9 to 5: Men and Women at Work.* William Morrow, 1994.

———. *You Just Don't Understand: Men and Women in Conversation.* William Morrow, 1990.

Twist, Lynne. *The Soul of Money: Transforming Your Relationship with Money and Life.* W. W. Norton, 2003.

Warren, Elizabeth, and Amelia Warren Tyagi. *The Two-Income Trap: Why Middle-Class Parents Are Going Broke.* Basic Books, 2003.

Wolaner, Robin. *Naked in the Boardroom: A CEO Bares Her Secrets So You Can Transform Your Career.* Fireside, 2005.

ACKNOWLEDGMENTS

THIS BOOK WOULD NOT EXIST WITHOUT THE GENEROUS contributions of the nearly two hundred anonymous and pseudonymous women who agreed to be interviewed and who shared their rich and fabulous lives so enthusiastically. I am also indebted to the many experts—especially Juliet Schor, Jean Chatzky, Chellie Campbell, Ann Crittenden, Barbara Stanny, Deborah Tannen, Pamela York Klainer, Stephen Goldbart, Joline Godfrey, and Dr. Louann Brizendine—whose experience and wisdom shed so much light.

I thank Jim Steyer, Susan Sachs, Beth Pratt, and the rest of the Common Sense Media staff for their patience and understanding as I juggled work and writing.

To the divine Richard Pine and Lori Andiman, thank you seems too weak for what you've done for me. Sue Wels and Dave Hagerman, my dearest friends of four decades, thank you for all that and especially for putting up my son and me for five months when we were homeless. Jane Isay, Leslie Schnur, Lisa Queen, Carole Bidnick, Karen Laughlin, Lisa Okuhn, and Robin Wolaner informed this manuscript in more ways than I can say. I offer them my heartfelt thanks for reading, critiquing, keeping me honest, and helping me think straight.

Jennifer Barth proves that there are still editors devoted to their authors and their craft and who know how to edit. To Sam Douglas, Maggie Richards, and John Sterling, my gratitude for welcoming me into their publishing house and making me feel at home.

My ex-husband, Steve, has been supportive in all ways, including encouraging me to tell this story. It turns out he was right. We are better off as friends.

Finally, to my family. My thanks go to my father, Gabe Perle, for just about everything. David and Roshann, I am so grateful to you for being such wonderful people. Steve Pressman, my husband, you are a brilliant editor, writer, and companion. How on earth did I ever get so lucky?

You all have truly made me a wealthy woman indeed.

INDEX